Selected Quotes By Author from the Poems

"Live your dreams, be your best and lead a life worthy of your invaluable birth"

*"Love is holding of trust, not merely clasping of hands.
It's two hearts that beat as one throughout"*

*"Love is something but seems like nothing.
Love is not anything but everything"*

*"A woman is the greatest gift to man as mother, wife and daughter.
She is an embodiment of love and epitome of motherhood"*

*"A man is charmed by what he sees, a woman by
what she hears, until they come down to earth,
only to find where infatuation has taken them"*

*"Marriages shake if threatened, worse if betrayed.
All issues can be resolved if the spark is kept alive.
Won't just sincerity and trust bind two to eternity?"*

*"Knowledge is derived from all forms of study;
Wisdom is knowledge, experience and soul search"*

*"Life is full of uncertainties and suspense.
Only the wise brace against changes and shocks"*

*"The human being with superior intellect, articulate speech
and upright stance is the most astounding earthly being"*

*"In the chart of lives what an amazing
and unique creation man is"*

"Whatever you endeavor to accomplish, do it in style and make a difference"

S. Errakiah

Selected Quotes By Author
from the Poems

"Out of conflict without we wrestle; out of conflict within we feign to be philosophers"

*"A politician dramatizes and even cups one's tears
in his hands for he is the greatest actor of all times"*

*"Nuclear weapons in the hands of lunatics and
unscrupulous leaders will prompt the doomsday"*

*"Regret not the past, yesterday is experience;
Fret not the future, tomorrow is suspense;
Waste not the present, today is your chance"*

*"With no more trees and fruits; greens and grains;
rivers and fishes ;cattle and fowls; clean water
and fresh air; what else can keep us alive"*

*"Little does man realise, the supreme he prays to
is the very energy that reigns the hills, forests,
seas and rivers that he ruthlessly ruins"*

*"The only way to come out a winner from a
casino is by crushing the urge to gamble on"*

*"Destinies are puppets in the grasps of preordained fates.
Attachments are puppets in the clasps of mortal bondage"*

*"Losers admit defeat and readily retreat;
Winners persist and fight all the way to the last"*

*"Success is bouncing back from momentary defeats
to contend again and again till you attain"*

"It's not riches or luxuries but memories of moments that ultimately matter in life"

S. Errakiah

Reflections
of a
Dreamer

Life. Love. Learning. Wisdom. Wealth. Winning. Happiness.
Global Warming. Climate Change. Pollution. Puppets. Gaming.
Poverty. Debts. Wars. Miracle. Divinity. Faith. Almighty. Death.

Errakiah Sannasi

Edited and Illustrated by
Girijah Balakrishnan

PARTRIDGE

Print information available on the last page.

To order additional copies of this book, contact
Toll Free 800 101 2657 (Singapore)
Toll Free 1 800 81 7340 (Malaysia)
orders.singapore@partridgepublishing.com

Distributor: Global Eco Enthusiast, Malaysia.
email: ennierikka1707@gmail.com
Tel. 0192774776/ 60356338776/60356128776

Cataloging-in-Publication
Errakiah Sannasi, 1949-
Reflections of a Dreamer / by Errakiah Sannasi.
Revised Ed.
145 p. 23 cm.
ISBN: Softcover 978-1-5437-4009-7
         eBook   978-1-5437-4008-0
1. Malaysian poetry (English). 2. English poetry -- Malaysian authors.
3. Global warming--Environmental aspects. 4. Humanity. 5. Civilization.
6. Communities--Social aspect.

PR9530.6 Err 2017   899.281

www.partridgepublishing.com/singapore

Contents

*"Life is a call to souls to evolve and involve, not a bundle
of puzzles and problems to solve or resolve"*

"Go green; nurture nature; enliven the environment and live a lovely life"

"The best approach to this borrowed time, we call –
life is right now today not tomorrow"

*"We are all of one family and we belong to the one and only God.
We merely differ in our approaches of serving HIM"*

Dedication

Dedicated to my
Family:

Grandma / Naanamma
Mdm. Enni Atchammah
who was instrumental in initiating
my early education in an English school
in the 1950's, a privilege indeed
during the colonial era.

Caring parents : Sannasi and Akkammah
My inspiration, dear wife: Yogamalar
Affectionate daughter: Dr. Nalayeni Rao
Thoughtful son-in-law: Dr. Mathan Mohan
Loving sons: Srinivaasan Rao ; Jegatheson Rao
Lovely and pleasant daughter-in-law:Tan Sze Yin

"Affection and devotion keep a family together"

Acknowledgement

My utmost heartfelt thanks go to Mrs. Girijah Balakrishnan who has spent a great deal of time editing, flavoring and spicing up the verses in my book. Her ideas, views, suggestions and illustrations have indeed provided additional dimensions to my work. She stood by me all the way through with immeasurable patience enhancing the presentation and overall quality of this text. My sincere gratitude and appreciation for her relentless efforts to make this book a reality.

My profound gratitude to Mr. R. Ganasa Murthi, a service-oriented gentleman and humanitarian for writing the foreword for this text and also for being a pillar of crucial support especially in the later years of my career.

My deepest appreciation to Mr. Applasamy for encouraging me to persevere with this work and for being my source of inspiration all along my educational journey.

My sincere thanks and gratitude to Mr. Antony Gomez for reviewing my text and sharing his expertise to present the work in a precise and presentable manner.

My heartfelt thanks to Dr. Manimangai Mani for guidelines on poetry-verse writing. Her constructive proposals indeed have enhanced the overall quality of presentation.

My special thanks to Ms. Easwary Alahakone for going through the text thoroughly and diligently and further refining the verses. Her timely involvement and input particularly in the application of appropriate grammar is very much appreciated.

My whole-hearted thanks to Mrs. Arudsakhty Magendran for having taken time to make the relevant amendments that has enhanced the language used in this text.

My salutations to practitioners and spiritual proponents who wholeheartedly shared their knowledge and insight, which however, in no way reflect my perceptions and viewpoints on religious concepts of the Almighty, philosophies, strategies and practices.

I express my thanks to all the authors and publishers listed in the bibliography as well as to all the sources of reference that I'm unable to trace and acknowledge here.

Finally I thank the staff of Partridge for giving their best in the production of this text.

"Adam was the only man, when he said a good thing,
knew that nobody had said it before him"
-Anon

Foreword

R. Ganasa Murthi, Retired Director
International Languages Teacher Training Institute
Kuala Lumpur, Malaysia.

I first came to know Mr. 'Erik' as he was fondly called
when I was appointed Director of the Sri Kota Teachers
Training College, Kuala Lumpur, Malaysia which later
became the International Languages Teacher Training
Institute (IPBA) in 2000 AD. I found him a likeable
personality very much loved by staff and students. His
easy-going manners and his ability to mix with all people
regardless of race and colour caught my attention.

Erik has vast experience in the field of education as he has been serving as a graduate
lecturer and chief librarian for many years at the Teacher Training Colleges in
Malaysia till his retirement at IPBA as Head of the Department of Library Sciences
in 2005.

His philosophical approach to life and his intense thirst for knowledge, truth and
reality reveal a poetic nature which now he has with great effort and courage put
together in this book 'Reflections of a Dreamer'. He penned his thoughts vividly
with the intent of what he does best-educate people especially the inquisitive youth.

His enthusiasm and inspiration to express his views come from his keen observation
and understanding of the anxiety and tension in today's unscrupulous materialistic
world. He has touched on a variety of topics and handled contradicting, sensitive
issues without mincing words when it comes to criticism.

His attempt to awaken the general public from their dream world and portray the
real sinking world is indeed a timely effort to redress their indifference and apathy
to the surrounding hazards and catastrophes. Like a lighthouse, he reflects appalling
current environmental and social issues.

I take this opportunity to compliment Erik on his effort. It is my sincere hope that
he'll not stop at this but continue with his thoughtful verses as his works will add
lustre to this genre of Malaysian English literature. It will be a beacon that will
enlighten and make sense of our complicated life on earth.

"Work is Worship and Service is Prayer"

Preface

Wise people say, before you leave this world for good, leave behind a descendant for posterity, plant a seed, write a book or perform an exemplary act to make this ravaged earth a much better place. I subscribe to planting optimistic thoughts in young minds to evoke a sensible approach to daily life, to alert and awaken them to pressing issues in society hence make decisive shift in their perspective.

My love for writing took an interesting turn when I was drawn to poems, sayings, quotations and proverbs. As much as a picture is said to depict a thousand words, I realized these succinct expressions are crystallized wisdom of lifetime experience. No wonder they are often used to add charm to speeches, discourses and writings not only as an added value but to bring home important and convincing messages.

I've been on this mission for more than a decade resourcing and compiling materials that are close to my heart and passion. These words in my work reflect my thoughts and convictions mostly drawn from wisdom extracted from writings and presentations of renowned leaders and reputable scholars. My experiences and observations from different facets of my life have also played a significant role in shaping this text.

Many of the sayings and views in my book are familiar to you but when you turn all the pages and say "How true!" that is the moment we connect, for we share the same experience and interest. That's when my objective and mission are accomplished too. What is it that we can do in our lifetime to save all that is gifted to us on this planet?

Perhaps the answer lies in Charlie Chaplin's powerful speech rendered in the 1940's. "Greed has poisoned our world. We have lost our way. Machines have given us in abundance and have left us in want. Knowledge has made us cynical. Cleverness has made us hard and unkind. We think too much and dream too little. More than machinery we need humanity. More than cleverness we need gentleness and kindness"

I yearn to see the birth of a new joyful world free from vices, menaces and tribulations. We deserve to live a much more purposeful, peaceful and meaningful life on this planet.

Jan 2017   "God is the Playwright, His play is man"   Errakiah Sannasi

My Dream Machine

It was as if I were caught by some whirling typhoon
as I look back at my struggles and stumbles in life.
I should celebrate now that I no longer flounder
but I need someone to share and laud my thoughts.
Perhaps I should blot my experiences out as insignificant
but the more I ignore the more it fevers my blood.

I must put them down in writing – what writing?
Though familiar with writing forms and genres
my passion strips all adherence to stipulated rules.
So I privilege myself with a poetic license of my own
to express in the best way I know how, to access my reader
revealing all the leaves of my life without favour or prejudice.

All I ask of you…. Come explore my world of thoughts with me.

"Dreams are not those that we see in our sleep; they should be the ones that never
let us sleep"

- A.P.J. Abdul Kalam, Former President of India.

LIFE AND LEARNING

Quotes By Author

"Life is nothing but an illusion or maya
that takes you on a life-long pursuit of enlightenment.
When you stop, you discover you've been chasing a mirage"

"Life is like bubbles and ripples that appear and disappear in water.
It's real while you're living, false when you're leaving"

"Life is a laboratory of experiments that affect success and failure.
Keep trying again and again till you transform your setbacks to triumph"

"Life is already trying and tough.
Do not attempt to complicate it further and then complain about it"

"Life is all about preferences - what to hold on to and what to let go"

=================================

"Live as if you were to die tomorrow; learn as if you live forever"
Mahatma Gandhi

"Thousands of candles can be lit by a single candle and it will
not shorten or decrease in being shared"
Gautama Buddha

"Education is kindling the flame, not filling the vessel"
Socrates

"All the world is a stage
and all the men and women merely players.
They have their exits and entrances"
William Shakespeare

01

Life

*"Before we come to grips to understand life,
our entire life comes to an end"*

To those who fear, life is a horror tale
To those who blunder, it's a tragedy
For those who laugh, life is a comedy
For the passionate, it's a love story
Life is a novel.

Some people take on the part of a hero
Some do the role of the wicked villain
Others fill up the rest of the characters
While a great majority form the audience
Life is a play.

When you crash into a mirror, it cuts
If you polish it, it glitters and gleams
When you frown at it, it frowns back
If you smile at it, it returns the smile
Life is a reflection.

The apparent pool of water is a mirage
The closer you go, the quicker it vanishes
The image is, but just a shadow
The more you chase, the further it goes
Life is an illusion.

Life begins with a question mark
Drifts on with commas and semicolons
Shocks and astounds with exclamation marks
Finally, after all endeavour it ends with a full stop
Life is punctuated.

"The great act is in finding the balance in rhythm, harmony and order in ourselves"

02

Life Is A Balance

"Life is a formidable balance between extremes.
However thin you slice, there are two sides to it"

Life is neither all perfect nor flawed
It is sometimes real and at times illusive
Just pause, you'll perceive life's demanding package
Levelheadedness is what is required to attain a balance.

You had no time to smile or laugh out aloud
What has transformed at home, you have no notion
Your wife's cooking you savour with no compliment
Has it ever occurred, your spouse has feelings abound?

If you took stock of your existence right at this time
you'd realise you're a proud corporate warrior of fame
But in the family you play no man, husband or father
In time you will regret your lost years of family bonding.

Take time to stop and smell the rose in your garden bloom
Watch the sunset and the caterpillar turn into a free butterfly
Take a break and go for a holiday or a picnic with your family
Express your love to your kids, hug them and be there for them.

You need to strike a balance with family, work and self
Like a ballet dancer does with discipline, precision and grace
End of the day, it's quality of life that matters, with priorities
appropriately balanced physically, mentally and spiritually.

03

Take On Life

"It's not the years in your life but the life in your years that matters"

Life is about resisting temptation and anger
besides curtailing vice, avarice and greed
Man has tamed animals and taken nations
He has mastered everything except himself
It is discipline.

Some fortunate ones swim across to safety
Others struggle and drown along the way
Time does not conclude the race for the victor
nor does it close the contest for the loser
It is a challenge.

The frugal few are the smart, mighty lenders
The imprudent lot, the miserable borrowers
Affluence and power bestowed on the former
Misery and destitution thrown on the latter
It is materialism.

Life is about returning favours for support
You flatter me and I will praise you to glory
Every action is inspired by a hidden motive
My turn today and clearly yours tomorrow
It is a bargain.

Prudence and security in all endeavor
is truly a matter of timing and mere chance
as in business investment, match or marriage
They can neither be guaranteed nor reassured
It is a gamble.

04

Take Life Easy

"How can you capture and study life that flees with time?"

Life is one undertaking after another
A nonstop chase after dreams and vision
No man is able to prevent the tough calling
Nor accomplish all things desired in smooth sailing.

Life is a series of changing targets
A challenge to excel and keep excelling
Every day is a new day to be made better
Inventing and innovating ways to the top.

Life is full of uncertainties and suspense
Nothing precise like prophesies of the stocks
varying weather and man's whims and fancies
Only the wise brace against changes and shocks.

Life is one long tedious, involving process
tussling and sparring with its illusive shadows
It's a cycle of unending beginnings that sprout
from every ending, groping to an unknown end.

Life is a struggle from womb to tomb
Neither resist nor be attached to it forever
You can strive and strain to remain here long
Rejoice all that you have amassed, but to no avail.

05

Education Is Life

"The failure of education is the downfall of man and his nation.
The fundamental challenge of education is to enlighten man"

Education is not merely filling facts in a head
or gleaning and storing information in the mind
Perhaps saved in memory for a proud declaration
but a mere prescription for survival in this world.

Education fortifies the spirit to resist dominance
and neither bungles nor buckles under pressure
It drives the will to persevere in order to attain
and gain wisdom to discern virtues from vices.

Education fosters and instills values to bring out
the best in a person when making wise decisions
and fair evaluation; with right attitude and approach
from a developed, decent and fortified mind.

Education is hardly the scaffolding of life
It is the acceptance of challenges and changes
More importantly a progressive, enduring journey
A realisation on how vast our ignorance is.

Education is essentially a tool for transformation
in today's world of information technology
It's wholesome education that enriches livelihood
The ultimate aspiration of education is knowing thyself.

06

A Teacher's Wish

*"A teacher prods and pushes and even jabs to lift the student
to the next plateau"*

I'm a teacher by wish and choice
In caring and sharing I rejoice
I want to impart to the students all that I know
to equip and enable them to develop and grow.

I wish to ignite interest for reading
thirst for books, knowledge and learning.
I plan to instill in them a sense of accountability
Naturally it comes with responsibility.

I wish to steer them to what is right
whether they are totally dull or bright
I want to do everything within my capacity
fortify their will to withstand any form of adversity.

I have no favourite, as I care for all
I have no black sheep for I love them all
I'm not in this profession to orate or preach
I do not want to just teach, but essentially reach.

Employing wisdom to discern right over wrong
Armed with truth I prepare them firm and strong
All these I will continue to do to give them a good start
Then professionally and conscientiously I've done my part.

Tribute to a Teacher

Mr. S Applasamy
"You are remembered and cherished for your modesty and humility."

07

A Noble Profession

(Dedicated to Mr. S. Applasamy)

*"A teacher's fundamental role is sharing knowledge
and inculcating life's values"*

Being a teacher is most trying
Yet one of the noblest of all professions
A teacher's service is indeed fundamental
for the preparation of students for all careers.

Teaching is an art that molds students
designed on specific sets of curriculum
as precisely prescribed by the Government
They emerge stamped with allegiance to the state.

Information technology deletes tradition
The chalk, board and class become obsolete
Compassionate inspiring role models turn to fiction
A know-all educator and dictator, virtual supersedes.

Teaching is demanding and tedious as may be
Patience, tolerance and enthusiasm you see
Lest interest expire, inspire the wilted to retrieve
Many resolve to teach but only some do achieve.

A good teacher nudges you to tag on to hope
A passionate teacher ignites imagination to innovation
A great teacher designs the mold to befit the students' aptitude
A born teacher is an artist and his medium is forever evolving.

08

I Am Knowledge

*"The knowledgeable differ from the ignorant as the sighted
differ from the blind"*

I'm the light that dispels the darkness around you
I'm the sight that opens up the world to you
I'm the compass that shows you the direction
I'm the map that guides you all along the way.

Kings are recognized only within boundaries
But I'm adored in all corners of the world
The seas too, rise and fall within their shores
I practise neither restrictions nor limits.

I have no fear of being robbed or taken away
I don't wear out clean, however much utilised
The more I am used, the more I top you up
I'm growth and progress and never ending.

I shrink not with criticism or swell with praise
Neither do I dissolve in water nor melt in fire
I am for life and not transient or ephemeral
I'm indeed the very breath and life of mankind.

I am a priceless and an invaluable treasure
But ignorance hurts and is even more costly
When I'm embraced and utilised, you will live
If I'm ignored or shunned, you will merely exist.

09

Wisdom And Knowledge

"Wisdom is the quintessence of knowledge and experience"

Knowledge is information discovered and assimilated
Wisdom is application of information from knowledge
Knowledge accrues facts packed orderly in one's mind
Wisdom enables one to act rationally with facts internalized.

Knowledge fortifies and strengthens the brain and mind
Wisdom equips one's capacity to make the right judgment
Knowledge merely endows, educates and empowers to live
Wisdom enlightens and enables one to live a meaningful life.

Knowledge is the essential ingredient for decision making
Wisdom is pondering and experiencing the absolute truth
Knowledge is realised by observing and taking things apart
Wisdom is grasping, analyzing and putting things together.

Knowledge can be attained by him who seeks it earnestly
Wisdom comes to him who is knowledgeable and sensible
Knowledge is derived from all forms of study and education
Wisdom comes with knowledge, experience and soul search.

Knowledge supplements and fortifies the mind to act wisely
Wisdom is enriched with continuous exposure to knowledge
Knowledge enhances the faculty of wisdom in human beings
Wisdom develops and strengthens with growth of knowledge.

*"A mother's arms are made of tenderness
and children sleep soundly in them"
- Victor Hugo 1802-1885*

10

Parents' Gift Of Love

"Our children yearn for our presence more than presents.
Be there with them for them"

You needn't take them to fun fairs and operas
but inject in them confidence and guts
You needn't treat them to clubs and cafes
but instill in them virtues and values.

You needn't put them on cruises and flights
but show them dewdrops and fireflies
You needn't buy them roller skates for winter
but raise them with faith and character.

You needn't purchase them expensive attire
but shower onto them true love and care
You needn't get them emeralds and pearls
but inculcate in them integrity and ethics.

You needn't invest for them in stocks and shares
but encourage them to explore into ventures
You needn't leave them a wealthy will to inherit
but prepare them to excel on the basis of merit.

You needn't gather for them valuable collections
but train them to make proper decisions and choices
You needn't install for them, luxurious Home Theatres
but make them realise they're treasured in your hearts.

LOVE AND LOYALTY

Quotes By Author

"True love is not merely physical or spiritual but acceptance
of everything that was, is and will be"

"Love, sweet love entering through the eyes and ears
melts the affectionate heart"

"Riches and resources amassed by a man mean nothing
if they are not meant for his beloved woman"

"Being sensitive to likes and dislikes may help save marriage"

"With a compatible spouse you'll be merry.
With a mismatched spouse you'll be weary.
When you're totally disillusioned you'll be dreary"

"Sexual lust when uncontrolled is a wild horse without a bridle.
It has to be very well contained, tamed and reined"

=========================

"...were beauty under twenty locks kept fast
yet love breaks through and picks them all at last"
William Shakespeare

"A man wants to be a woman's first love,
a woman wants to be his last"
Oscar Wilde

11

Love

"Love looks not with eyes or mind but with a loving heart"

Love is a joyful emotion
that none can try to hide
Just a glimpse would suffice
and even silence will reveal
Love is a universal feeling.

Love is for all
The blind can see it
The deaf can hear it
The dumb can express it
Love is a global language.

Love bows not to logic
Love makes pretty follies
Wits and reason take flight
Love blossoms out of the blues
Love is like grapes of passion.

Love is a burning flame
inspired by a passionate desire
It's a short pleasure, thrill and fun
ending up with long term commitment
Love is a conviction.

A man is charmed by beauty
A woman is delighted by sweet words
Until they both come down to earth only
to find where infatuation has taken them
Love is fascination.

"Women are made to be loved, not understood"
- Oscar Wilde

12

Anything For Love

"True love alters not, bends not nor abandons
but survives catastrophe"

Over the steepest rocks
Through the deepest floods
Against the roughest waves
Down the darkest dungeons.

Climb the hills, I will
just to hear your voice
Cross the rivers, I will
to feel your tender touch.

Walk miles afar, I will
just to see your smile
Face any challenge, I will
to see you safe and sound.

Bear any pain, I will
just to stay by your side
Wait however long, I will
to make you just my own.

Trust me wholeheartedly
However rough the journey
Say no matter what or how
I will surely be there for you.

"Cupid is a knavish lad, thus to make poor females mad"
- W. Shakespeare

13

Woman's Nature

"A woman's heart is as unfathomable as the ocean
and unpredictable as the weather"

A woman is predominantly known
for her gaiety, vanity, frailty and finery
More often possessive, fickle minded
insatiable and at times even merciless.

When a woman hears a man just say
she's pretty and she's his very breath
she turns as blank as an empty bottle
far too dizzy to see all his other lies.

She believes whatever she hears
With no second thought rushes
into a relationship, head over heals
just to regret and retreat thereafter.

The love of a woman is known to be
very beautiful but also quite fearful
Sometimes she is as calm as the sea
At times she explodes like a volcano.

No matter what, it is beyond man
to fathom a woman's mysterious ways
as she wheels her wandering mind but
unfailingly guards the man in her heart.

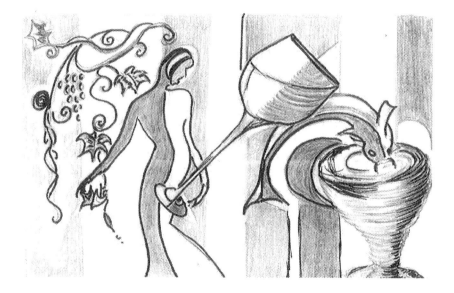

"Love like wine gets better with time"
- Anon

14

Macho Man

*"Many a man will dare to vanquish the formidable
for the love of a woman"*

Man born to a woman
is a dependent species
who is always in need
of a woman by his side.

He's able to mediate
with absolute discipline
But his eyes rove
as a woman's hips move.

He's hard as a steel cable
and firm as a crab's grip
But seeing a woman's tears
he melts like an ice cream.

He'll take the world
when he's challenged
But falls flat like a pancake
with a woman's sweet smile.

Man is still not capable of
fathoming a woman's heart
for he turns silly as a goose
in the presence of a woman.

"Speak low if you speak of love"
    - W. Shakespeare

15

A Sweet Torment

"By all means fall in love and go through hell and heaven"

Love is bitter yet sweet and soothing
Love is sacrifice yet selfish and possessive
Love is anxiety but thrilling and exciting
Love is forgiving yet blaming and accusing.

Love is disappointing yet hopeful and confident
Love is tolerance but demanding and nagging
Love is deceptive yet true and sincere
Love is real but with infatuation and illusion.

Love is fire but cool and comforting
Love is faith but with despair and skepticism
Love is jealousy yet with admiration and adoration
Love is submission yet obstinate and impatient.

Love is passion yet kind and compassionate
Love is trust but with doubts and suspicion
Love is lust but with fun and fulfillment
Love is paradise yet torture and hell.

Love is a burden but with bliss and felicity
Love is divine yet cruel and vindictive
Love is something but seems like nothing
Love is just not anything but indeed everything.

"Time passes but true love endures"

16

True Love Endures

"First love never dies"

Love is sharing and enduring
It's not nagging or demanding
Love is simple, natural and eternal
not fickle, fictional nor conditional.

Love is a deep feeling inside
not a lustful craving when beside
Love is an active emotion and passion
not a momentary charm nor admiration.

Love is an everlasting feeling
and not merely clasping of hands
It's two minds with the same thought
Two hearts that beat as one throughout.

In loneliness lovers are down
In happiness their souls awaken
They who sincerely love each other
indeed bind their body and soul forever.

True love chooses not cottages nor palaces
It neither hastens nor wearies but patiently waits
It is the joy of love that makes the world go round
Love is indeed an invaluable gift unique to man alone.

"If I had a flower for every time I thought of you,
I could walk through my garden"
- Alfred Tennyson

17

Greatest Gift To Man

"In God's creation a woman is a prodigy on the
pedestal for posterity"

God's most enchanting marvel on this
planet is none other than a woman
Her hair, her eyes, her cheek, her lips
her poise, her grace and her elegance.

A marvelous creation, symbol of beauty
an epitome of love is still a woman
There's in her cheer, joy, love, patience
and all the essence of heavenly paradise.

There isn't another equal to this damsel
Her sweet voice, her pleasing smile
her charming glances that have lured
and tempted many a saint and rulers.

She's loving, she's affectionate
She's caring, she's compassionate
She's inspiration, she's fulfillment
She's charming, she's delightful, she's life.

She's God's greatest gift to man
as mother, wife and daughter and there's
none to replace her except another woman
She's everything to man, his dream, his world.

"The institution of marriage is not for trial but for life"

18

Save Your Marriage

*"A lasting marriage is when a couple come together and learn
to accept their differences"*

In a beautiful relationship blooms a marriage
A man and a woman meet in mutual agreement
to raise a loving family as nature needs fulfillment
the very basis for the existence of society.

Marriages many believe are fixed in heaven
In reality they're nurtured on the corporeal earth
Remember you aren't any more a single haven
Another has now become your life long concern.

One forgives and forgets to the extent one loves
chooses to live without any prods or prompts
Marriages shake if threatened, worse if betrayed
All other matters can be fixed, the spark kept alive.

Marriage isn't just love and pleasurable cherishes
Should it flounder with the question of equality
or swoon to respect, compromise and sacrifice
Won't just sincerity and trust bind two to eternity?

The creator of mankind ensured human survival
The institution of marriage assured continuance
The families of the couple offered the pivotal role
Whither could one divorce a plan so awesome in life?

WINNING AND VICTORY

Quotes By Author

An Enterprise to an Empire:
"In the year 1599 a group of businessmen met at London and initiated
a small trading enterprise with a capital of about 100,000 pounds.
This gave rise to the historical East India Trading Company which
attained the status of an imperial power playing a fundamental
role in the British overseas expansion for two and half centuries
until its demise with the upheaval of the Indian Mutiny in 1857"
-History

"It's not so much, how many times you win in life,
but winning 'life' itself that matters most in life"

"Integrity and ingenuity are the indispensable ingredients of
innovation and inventions"

"It's not just your word or action but the approach and attitude
that draw others to your leadership"

"A man should keep his: vision and mission in the forefront;
letdowns and washouts behind; contenders and enemies at a distance;
but his wife beside to attain greater heights of success in his endeavours"

=====================================

"I can give a six-word formula for success:
"Think things through - then follow through"
Edward Rickenbacker

"Victory is Spirit" - Anatole France

19

Visualise to Realise

"A dream remains a dream until an effort is made to make it a reality"

When you're facing a trying contest
imagine you've survived, you'll thrive
When you're playing in a tournament
imagine you've outshined, you'll succeed.

When you're running a tough race
imagine you've overwhelmed, you'll win
When you're fighting a crucial battle
imagine you've prevailed, you'll triumph.

When you're facing a formidable task
imagine you've overcome, you'll finish it
When you're taking a fabulous challenge
imagine you've realized it, you'll accomplish.

When you're writing a qualifying exam
imagine you've excelled, you'll attain it
When you're attending an interview
imagine you have aced you'll be selected.

When you're wooing a charming damsel
imagine you've won, she will be yours
When you're chasing an invaluable treasure
imagine you have possessed it, you'll procure it.

20

Think To Triumph

"Clarity in thought is the basis of realization of a vision"

Thinking like feeling and breathing
has got to be done all by yourself
The greatest gift to the human race
is the ability to think and rationalise.

You've to dream before you imagine
Ponder deeply prior to deciding
One with a vivid vision and direction
thinks before he decides and acts.

Many a man avoids deep thinking
It's the hardest thing to indulge in
Trials alone do not ensure triumphs
Planning and executing assure victory.

Look ahead before you leap lest
you trip, tumble and fall in the pit
Think very intensely before you act
so that you make decisions right.

It's thinking alone that clearly makes
the fundamental difference between
the intellectual and the instinctive
the human being and the wild beast.

21

Get Organised

"Discipline and diligence will transform man's action to excellence"

Not that I'm frivolous or playful
Not that I'm sluggish or slothful
I do this and that with all my might
Yet I'm unable to finish what I am at.

Whatever I put my hands on
I attempt as hard as anyone can
The day is soon coming to an end
Yet, my gracious! I get so little done.

My work seems to pile into a heap
It bothers me a lot even in my sleep
What I lack is a scheme and a system
Only then can I finish my work on time.

I've still got so much to complete
I really do not know where to start
If only I can get myself well organized
I'll do much more, you will be amazed.

Alas, I realise I've to focus carefully
Handle one thing at a time patiently
Work rightly, assessed and measured
certainly it can be addressed and settled.

Reach high for stars hidden in you. Dream deep,
for every dream precedes the goal"
- Rabindranath Tagore

22

Act To Achieve

"Go-getters would rather embark on new horizons of challenge rather than trail on worn out paths of prospects"

A dream without action is but a mere fantasy
Visualising is not just entertaining of thoughts
It's planning and putting them all into action
Achievement comes with doing, not wishing.

Victory begins with a vision and a conviction
followed by consistent and persistent action
Performance is worth more than mere advice
Action and result speak louder than mere words.

Desire and passion pump in energy for action
and as one thinks, plans and acts, he becomes
Focus attentively on the mission undertaken
Success is in doing well what you are doing.

Success is resilience and bouncing back from
the brink of momentary defeat and setback
to contend over and over again till you attain
Winning comes with extraordinary enthusiasm.

You have got to go all out, until you are all in
It's standing upright and firm to be counted in
Whatever the task, do it and make a difference
Excellence means second to none, but the best.

23

Prepare And Pursue

"One's strife and strike should be timely
to hit the target precisely"

Victory comes to him
who is always prepared
It embraces him readily
when opportunity knocks.

Get your winter coat
well before the season
Winter is surely coming
sooner or later.

Dig not the well
only when driven thirsty
You will never be able
to get the water in time.

No amount of remorse
can redress losses
Do it right the first time
on time, and at all times.

The cautious and skeptical
ponder and hesitate
They fear all the way
The prepared, bravely pursue.

24

Begin Right Now

*"Procrastination keeps tomorrow at bay.
Readiness and willingness pave the way for performance"*

Look not back nor grieve the bygone past
It's merely running water under the bridge
If you hold on tight to the finished past
you can't best utilise the present in hand.

Do not be troubled by the time ahead
It's merely a journey into the unknown
If you wish to live the beautiful present
worry not about the unpredictable future.

Reflecting the past and fearing the future
destroy not the precious present with you
Today in fact is the future that you were
concerned and worried about yesterday.

Regret not the past, yesterday is experience
Fret not the future, tomorrow is suspense
Waste not the present, today is your chance
Within past and future, now is performance.

Life is not mere inquiry or enquiry but action
Perform today as if there is no tomorrow
There is no such thing as trying or tarrying
It's just 'do' or 'don't do', and that's about all.

"Step by step and always at it,
Turns a piece of work into a masterpiece"

25

One Step At A Time

"We are what we repeatedly execute and accomplish"

The marathon runner paces his run
till he reaches the distant finish line
A step at a time with hearty endurance
even a formidable task is surmounted.

The turtle begins to progress forward
when it sticks its neck out into the open
The only possible way to receive a ship
Is by launching one into the open sea.

A green worm-like fat caterpillar
transforms into a colourful butterfly
The tiny finger length baby joey grows
into a sizeable large galloping kangaroo.

Winning comes with a step at a time
always beginning with the first step
Winners persist and fight till the last
while losers admit defeat and retreat.

The idea of life isn't mere existence
but living with a purpose and direction
Take one day and one thing at a time
Set your target, focus and begin right away.

"Losers give up and surrender; winners endure and accomplish

26

Be A Winner Always

"Let not your victory get to your head!
Move on, for there is yet another race to run"

A winner visualizes, schedules and performs
A loser broods, daydreams and withdraws
A winner has ideas, programs and strategies
A loser has excuses, complaints and doubts.

A winner is a doer who targets and achieves
A loser is a dreamer who lazes and relaxes
A winner devises and maneuvers his moves
A loser roams aimlessly without any plans.

A winner comes out stronger from his failures
A Loser grieves and gripes about his setbacks
A winner strives and thrives in daunting crisis
A loser tumbles and shatters in tough times.

A winner explores new frontiers and horizons
A loser trails on norms and age old traditions
A winner goes along with times and changes
A loser is slack and generally behind times.

A winner is a part of answers and solutions
A loser is a part of skepticisms and objections
A winner thinks, resolves, and accomplishes
A loser lingers, wavers, dilly-dallies and tarries.

POLLUTION AND POSTERITY

Quotes By Author

"An unscrupulous politician has neither noble ideologies nor ideal philosophies but merely personal interests and insatiable desires"

"In today's politics, victory in elections is apparently not in the voting alone but more crucially in the counting"

"Corruption has penetrated considerably, all nooks and corners of the world. Nothing is spared by its tempting baits and carrots"

"The despicable minority is comfortably riding on the docile majority. Dodgy leaders manipulate and manoeuvre innocent masses"

"Natural calamities have become a global crisis that warrants remedies. Clean energy revolution is crucial to combat the devastating climate bomb"

"It's time for awareness in the general populace, specially the indifferent lot who are still in a daze over the haze prevalent in the atmosphere"

"A world free of pollution and nuclear armaments are today's two topmost priorities for a healthier and safer life"

=======================

"The Alarm Bells are ringing. We can't pretend we are not hearing. We have to answer the call" - New York, 2014
"Never have been stakes so high. It's probable to go green without wrecking economic growth" – Paris, 2015
Climate Change Summits - Barack Obama, Former President, USA

"There are two times in a man's life, when he should not speculate: when he can't afford it and when he can" --Mark Twain

"It's time we reverse, might is right to right is might" --Abraham Lincoln

27

Indifferent To Differences

*"We can live sometimes without relatives but not all by ourselves
without neighbours or friends"*

There are indeed differences among people around the world
But indifference makes all the differences in the people
Perhaps it's the differences that bring out variety in mankind
On the flip side, indifference merely leads to dark ignorance.

With some difference, people differentiate colour and creed
But indifference flavours prejudice and pre-judgment
Like one half of the world is in the dark and the other bright
it's indifference more than the difference that tends to split us.

Absence of interaction amongst people is the single factor
for creation of distant neighbours' in most residencies today
Just like water all round a sailor in the sea, with no drop to sip
people all around, but not a single soul to assist in times of need.

Some escalate to the pinnacle of fame and authority
Others in spite of all the struggle and effort, go down the lane
No matter how different or remote, the crux of the matter is that
people different or indifferent seem to remain on their own planes.

What difference have discoveries and inventions made
Man remains indifferent oblivious of others as he builds his pylons
Lofty perceptions display indifference to others' pains and losses
On a different stroke has man considered reconstructing himself?

TREE OF LIFE

"When trees fall man falls"
- Chinese Saying 1876-1916

28

Climate Warning

"Man battling fellow man either defeats or gets defeated.
Man at war with nature is himself the ultimate casualty"

From the dawn of time man has remained hostile to mother nature
Ungrateful for the home she has provided, unappreciative of her natural
gifts and beauty, and unrepentant, despite her repeated warnings
How audacious of man to tear open the earth as if he could dictate it?

The beauty of our planet and its magical balance is repeatedly disrupted
by unscrupulous acts of man which provoke monstrous natural calamities
The earth has been stripped, raked and depleted of its natural resources
for reasons couched, in the name of development and civilization.

When mother earth rises with fury she strikes mercilessly whipping up
severe catastrophic calamities - super storms, heat waves and flash floods
None of man's discovery or tools of technology can combat that power
Act fast we must before all species are wiped out from this planet.

We are indeed responsible for what we have reduced the world today
We want clean air and water, our climates that were once so predictable
All the endangered species are protected and returned to their habitat
Most of all we want to be part of nature and enjoy the harmony.

We owe it to our future generation to redeem the desired pristine world
with admirable unity in diversity maintained as sustainable existence
For God's sake stand up for this ravaged earth with all your heart and might
Love and care for mother earth as you would love and care your own.

29

Global Warming

Natural calamity is a testimony to nature's power provoked"

All things in this universe and the world are uniquely connected
Forests, hills, seas, rivers, all species including animals
and the human race are invaluable gifts of the Almighty God
created with a purpose best known only to Him.

The Earth has been warming since the last century
a result of climate change brought about by greenhouse effects
Alarming levels of global warming, the most devastating menace
to mankind, urges to be addressed very urgently.

Human race is now in a daze over consistent haze spewed by
blazing forest fires, carbon pollutants from age old factories
Smoke belching vehicles, overwhelm the environment
Does anybody care how, laden with pollution, we choke?

Nuclear tests in oceans, excessive emission of carbon dioxide
and merciless acidity, wipe out coral reefs and marine life
Rockets and satellites invade, not even the outer space is spared
The ozone layer collapses exposing mankind to harmful radiation.

Greenland, Antarctica land ice, world glaciers and Ice bergs
are breaking and melting, flowing into the vast oceans
All these with the shrinking of the Arctic sea have caused the rise
of sea levels, resulting in the submergence of low lying Islands.

The abusive acts of man towards the environment and nature
have resulted in severe reaction of nature hitting back
with catastrophic natural calamities of super storms
intense rainfall, landslides, heat waves and flash floods.

Greenhouse effects and consequent climate change leading
to acute droughts and massive floods have caused severe
crop failures and demise of livestock thus resulting in food crisis
Affected farmers are now pushed to poverty and suicide.

Global warming warrants instant remedies of recycling
cleaning up rivers, restoring landscapes, conserving forests
and most of all stabilizing: the equilibrium of the ecosystem
climate and mankind; the reciprocity between man and nature.

Is man privileged to dominate and affect the destruction of
this fabulous planet and the invaluable species and life in it?
As humanitarians voice for the survival of the human race
politicians have to make tough choices to save this ravaged earth.

With no more: trees and fruits; rivers and fishes; cattle and fowls
greens and grains; crops and harvests; provisions and groceries
clean water and fresh air; what on this earth can keep us all alive?
Salutations to the innovator of hydro, wind and solar alternative energies.

"In all things of nature there's something of the marvelous"
- Aristotle

30

Mystical Nature

"Sunshine and rainfall are bestowed alike upon all mankind but wherever man lands, he avariciously and vehemently claims it as his own property"

Wonderful nature with what beauty! what mystery! what a palette of colours!
Each time the flowers, dry leaves and withered petals drop, it fascinates
Nature generates, regenerates, vitalizes, revitalizes and nurtures fresh ideas
Is man not an amazing creation yet a link in the same cycle?

The winds carry the scent of the flowers embalming the air with fragrance
The green boughs of trees bend, laden with swollen fruit in the offering
Busy bees and insects in drunken mode hover in circles with pollen shoes
Should the beauty of this world be forgotten or forsaken by man?

Hasn't man experienced the first scent of a rose, the fascination of twilight,
the thrill of the birth of dawn, the serenity of a clear sky, the soothing breeze
and the yellow bird flitting among the palms singing praise of the berries
Why does man blind himself with the desire to destroy for transient riches?

Man changed the earth, stripping hills and constructing high rise structures
Ironically man prays to the Supreme Being, little realising the supreme energy
reigns the mountains, forests, oceans and rivers, that he ruthlessly ruins
If he truly believed in the Supreme Being, would he terrorize and devastate?

Why does man not rave and rejoice - the sway of flowers in the wind
the beat of waves on rocks, the flutter of butterflies from blossom to blossom
relish - the whirl of the ripples on the pool, the couched dewdrops on petals
the drizzle on hollows, the rivers in cascade and the glow of sunset on mountains?

"Bullies are mere 'survivors' masquerading as winners among those reduced to puppets"

31

A World Of Puppets

*"We are but mere transient puppets dancing to the forces
of preordained destinies"*

The good are puppets in the hands of the bad
The weak are puppets in the hands of the tough
The naive are puppets in the hands of the cunning
The innocent are puppets in the ploys of the swindlers.

The patriots are puppets in the grips of the ruler
The followers are puppets in the grips of the leader
The devotees are puppets in the grips of the minister
The minorities are puppets in the grasps of the majority.

The poor are puppets in the clasps of the affluent
The borrowers are puppets in the clenches of loan sharks
The losers are puppets in the grasps of the jubilant winners
The juvenile are puppets in the grips of the adult delinquents.

Destinies are puppets in the clasps of preordained fates
Attachments are puppets in the clasps of mortal bondage
After all, lives are puppets in the clasps of inevitable death
In fact none has ever seen the Hands that manipulate the strings.

No puppet is invincible nor awakens to fight the illusion
So real, virtually very few realise the end game or purpose
Puppets spirited, play a mockery act: they on time enter; in time exit
Come to think of it, we are but mere predestined transient puppets.

"It takes just one crazy, narcissistic, lunatic Head to trigger a nuclear world war that will flatten the earth in seconds"

32

Mankind On Warpath

*"After a ravaging nuclear world war battles will be fought
with bows and arrows until history repeats itself"*

Cavemen and tribal rivalries, national and global wars
ruthlessly graved enormous innocent lives on this earth
These wars were fought under the claim of protecting
their nations least realising a war can't be ended with war.

Ancient kings and dictators like Alexander the Great
Napoleon Bonaparte, Adolf Hitler and Mussolini
made many conquests to bring the entire world
under their empires at the cost of huge armies.

The 20th century sadly witnessed ruthless killings of
lives with the dropping of devastating atomic bombs
Neither the League of Nations nor the United Nations
after two world wars have succeeded in civilising man.

The crusades to date have not come to a stop-
Jews clash with Palestinians in the Middle East
Muslims fight Hindus in the Indo - Pakistan border
Shiites against Sunnis and Protestants against Catholics.

Nuclear weapons of danger, extreme in the hands
of unscrupulous lunatic leaders prompt the doomsday
We are indeed sitting on a lethal time bomb that can be
triggered to explode any moment resulting in mass destruction
sparing no species, marvels or wonders on the face of the earth.

"If you must play, remember three things: the rules of the game;
the stake and the quitting time"

33

Gamble Never

*"If you have become a gambler, discover what it takes
to be a winner or do your utmost to quit it altogether"*

Betting is placed on Casino games, Slot machines
Horse racings, Jackpot lotteries, Sports matches
Online Internet games, Political Election results
Cock fights and many more bloodier competitions.

Gamblers dispense with cars, valuable ornaments and
even ATM cards as collateral in exchange for hard cash
to 'loan sharks', who await them eagerly to bite their
bait like hungry wolves, pouncing on vulnerable prey.

Currently, Online Internet gambling is the fastest
growing and most popular amongst the young
Its easy access with a few clicks, enables to operate
conveniently at all times from the home itself.

Big time criminals are patronizing illegal gaming dens
Burglary in homes and pickpocketing on streets rise
While betting and gambling are rampant and raging
What cost and suffering the gambler's family endure?

One sure way of coming out as an absolute winner
is when you're determined not to gamble any more
If you're hooked, just resist and put a stop to it altogether
If you haven't gambled at all, for heaven's sake don't start.

34

Entrapping Enticements

"Corruption is nurtured both by the beneficiary and benefactor"

Enticement is a mutual transaction that influences choices
and demands special favours of all kinds in exchange for
inducement, incentives, handouts, presents and privileges
Currently it has become a way of life in some communities.

For a long long time it used to be a powerful instrument
to lobby, influence and conclude only exclusive dealings
Presently it is pervading even into normal daily matters
as in the moving of files and beating a slow-moving queue.

Hard cash, rewards and treats of all types are extended
confidentially depending on the level of one's influence
One induces avaricious decision-making executives who
having no principles, ethics and morals, readily reciprocate.

Matches are no more sports but business fixed by punters
Recommendations from cronies surpass merit in selections
Promising remunerations affect favourable business deals
Even verdicts of judiciary are manipulated and manoeuvered.

What resolute action will the human race take to clean up
this escalating immoral activity or mess in the society today
Education with emphasis on values may be a slow but surely
the best bet, to save at least the future generations of the world.

35

A Fatal Affair

*"A moment of impulsive physical intimacy
culminates in lifetime distress and death"*

Those disco days, floating heads, dreamy eyes
Pretty girls in abandon, sliding bodies entice
The vision of sounds and taste of vivid colour
Promise a paradise of loveless sex set afire

Has the revengeful evil eye spotted me
Something sucks at my soul unyieldingly
Repulsive stares and deliberate shunning
My family! My blood! They too deserting.

I look at the mirror dirty and stained
Me? wispy hair, pale face, body maimed
My lifeless eyes hang barely in their cavity
A dire state screaming at this monstrosity.

Who would want to believe in my confession
As warned I am slain, absolutely no concession
Aids ; treacherous, unforgivable, breaks all ties
Will it deliver me alive to sickening worms, flies.

My one and only resort Mum….Dad….I miss you
I need one last hug and one last kiss as I bid adieu
Should I have known free love would be this fatal
Oh sweet death, I lie with you, an affair to end it all.

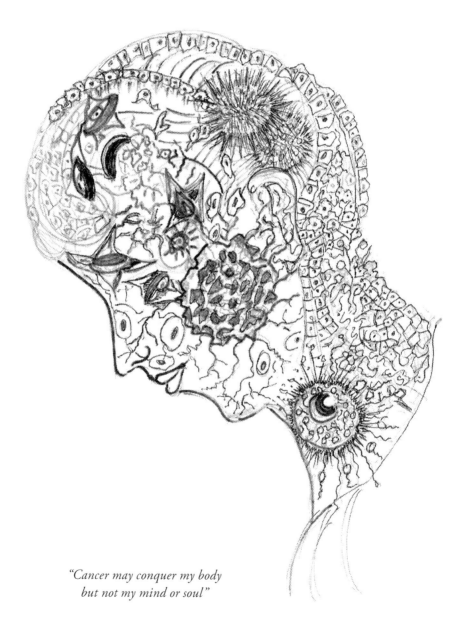

*"Cancer may conquer my body
but not my mind or soul"*

36

The No. 1 Killer

"Is cancer an instrument in the Divine's elimination process?"

The most feared, dreaded, unwelcome silent killer
a sneaky, impregnable terminator of ill-fated humankind
An unbearable persistent parasite that causes anxiety
instilling insecurity and despair in the agonized patients.

Its uncontrollable devious cells emerge unpredictable
posing a formidable challenge to modern medical science
Its precise nature or cause unknown and undisclosed
Medically calculated guesses point to unhealthy habits.

Is it a disease by mere chance or an infliction thrust on man
Are chemicals in preservatives and processed food the culprit
Perhaps it's nature's way of axing lives to maintain a balance
in the populace where modern medicine has raised lifespan.

Major breakthrough in medicine has given new hope
Findings in years of medical research which advanced
methods of treatment, have granted many a lease of life
Recovery is sometimes possible at an early stage of detection.

The diagnosis of cancer or this unmentionable disease
identified with caution is no more seen as a death sentence
Focus on this killer has become a priority over priorities
The man who made the lock obviously has the key to unlock it.
The battle goes on as with other critical diseases-this too will pass.

DEBTS AND DESTITUTION

Quotes By Author

"The poor toil to exist; the middle class cope with basic needs;
the rich live in comfort; the affluent float in luxury and high life"

"The wealthy are anxious about the end of life
while the meagre wage earners, the end of the day"

"The poor yearn for the money they can't get hold of.
The rich complain about the money they can't keep tight"

"When you splurge cash you have a crowd around you.
When you incur heavy debts you have to face the heat all alone"

"Man brings everything home to his dearest and closest.
It's time he shares the wealth he amassed, with the community"

=================================

"When it is a question of money everybody is of the same religion"
Voltaire

"A man who spends and saves money is the happiest man
because he has both enjoyments"
Samuel Johnson

"When I was young, I thought money was the most important thing in life;
now that I am old, I know that it is"
Oscar Wilde

37

Money Talks

*"When you're wealthy you're a bold, fearless lion.
When you're penniless you're a placid pond duck"*

Integrity was the way of life in olden times
Today it's money that activates the human
Money is winged to reach the sky and stars
Money sets the whole world in motion.

Your riches sound louder than a temple bell
When money opens its mouth, all is quiet
Money talks the lingo known to all people
Where gold speaks there is no more fight.

Money, a luxury surfer, wields absolute power
It invariably dances to the rich and wealthy
Even the sheep can sound like a roaring tiger
Being affluent is no more a sin but ingenuity.

Leaders make deals and nations sign pacts
Dealers extend gifts and incentives galore
Even priests practise favouritism in service
When it's money, people want more and more.

You cannot take it with you to sweet heaven
But where on earth can you go without it
A poor man's tale is never heard as ears deafen
A rich man's money talks, people listen. Doubt not.

"It's not the volume of money but the activity that counts"
- W. Bourke Cockran: 1854-1923

38

Money Flees

"We make a living with what we earn;
we make a remarkable life with what we share"

Money is merely an economic tool
It measures man's worth and status
Diligence earns this asset but greed
transforms it into the root of all evils.

Small accumulation of coins
end up in huge piles of notes
Like character and embroidery
money is made stitch by stitch.

Making money and honey is alike
bit by bit, day by day into a heap
You can make it with great effort
but it will never let you keep it.

Wind and fortune change fast
Money not only changes hand
but swiftly changes people too
Money! Here it is, there it flees.

When you don't have money
others aren't keen to know you
But when you possess lots of it
you don't want to know yourself.

"Debt so penetrates man with grief and humiliations"
- Charles Dickens

39

Grip Of A Loan

"Rather starve to death than live in never ending debt"

Debt is like a monitor lizard's grip
and just about as hard to get rid off
More often than not, a man in endless debt
is miserably trapped in a net his whole life.

Debts and diseases take away peace
Yesterday's luxuries are today's debts
He that borrows, has got to settle all of it
and very likely with great humiliation or loss.

When you borrow money from a bank
accrued interest with capital you rightly pay
When you borrow money from a friend
you lose his interest, without any say.

Ask your closest relative, a loan
You will then know how close, he is
You best weigh carefully, relative or friend
Determine well who you need more.

Just try borrowing to overcome a cost
Feigned sympathy you may get at the most
In life you're either a financial victor as a lender
or a wretched financial victim as a borrower.

40

Agony Of A Debtor

"The trauma of the indebted likens the agony of a waiting death"

A loan turns into a burden in most debtors' lives
as they dig new holes to close the earlier holes
In no time they find themselves heavily burdened
struggling to come out of them clean or unaffected
He that lives in debt, feels the pain and agony
a perpetual mental torture and anxiety.

You will be grieving once you go into borrowing
None can hear or sense your silent sobbing
It's a greater suffering and unbearable torture
wallowing in heavy debt than to be forever poor
Misfortune more often never comes singly
It never rains but pours unceasingly.

Patience and understanding is never the trend
nature or style of those who come forward to lend
Loans and unending debts cause dejection and worries
Loan sharks intimidate you like daunting menaces
Their unceasing demands, commands and pressure
leave you in severe tension and fear.

Banks and financiers issue notices and warrants
confiscate and auction your belongings
They won't hesitate to declare bankruptcy
for there is neither empathy nor sympathy
These can affect your serenity and peace
that are indispensable for you to convalesce with ease.

When you are trapped and squeezed in debt
your trusted contemporaries desert you flat
Friends unable to solve your excessive loan
inevitably leave you to face the heat alone
Your nearest and dearest, kith and kin leave
Your sweetheart and beloved ones promptly flee.

Debt like corrosive acid, drips on your pride
attracts none to assist or stand by your side
Like a chisel, it chips away your drive and morale
None to console you, not even the angel
It deprives you of your energy, spirit and vitality
depicting you as a man of poor integrity.

Being in debt is more cruel than death.
In its grip you die a thousand miserable deaths
When you are in destitution and in sizable debt
you can drop dead, that's your destiny or fate
The world isn't bothered if you survive or persist
die and inevitably be interred into dust.

When your promises and pledges aren't honoured
you remain mercilessly scorned and harassed
You can cry, plead, beg, vow, swear and assure
To rescue or salvage you not a single soul will dare
Alas! remember, it's only you and you alone care
You've to haul yourself out of this despicable snare.

"Poverty is the worst form of violence"
- Mahatma Ghandi

41

Poverty And Misery

*"Begging is no more a reflection of poverty
but an intimidating tool of extortion"*

Absolute poverty is a predicament indeed
A pathetic inability to satisfy basic needs
It is no vice nor disgrace to be in dire penury
Yet it's a violation of human dignity.

Poverty to man is breathing under water
Grabbing every little straw in desperation
Existing in misery in the grips of destitution
Not realising the inescapable cycle of scarcity.

Penury is not only being hungry, homeless
or naked but being unwanted and uncared for
Where ignorance prevails oppression takes over
to rob and degrade, instilling fear and stress.

The poor are more often ridiculed, slighted
and condemned for indolence, apathy and sloth
It's easy to give advice to overcome poverty
but extremely difficult and tormenting to bear.

Poverty is no disgrace or shame to moan
Born poor in circumstances best known
What's the excuse to remain poor all your life
Work hard, focus and press on to see the change.

42

Diligence Remunerates

*"Diligence, intelligence and resilience are the fundamentals
for successful accomplishment of a mission"*

The train of success runs on
the track of sturdy industry
Inspiration and ingenuity are
instrumental for innovation.

The most auspicious step
is still that out of the doors
A fisherman setting out for a
big catch hangs not in the shore.

No human can attain success
with his hands in the pocket
You cannot strike a ball with the
bat hanging on your shoulder.

No loaf is assured for a loafer
for there isn't any free meal
He who searches for diamonds
has to mine age-old coal.

It's definitely not the wishbone
but the backbone that yields
Destination of success is sweet
but its journey is full of sweat.

43

Spare And Spend

*"Spare when you are young and able,
to spend when you are old and feeble"*

Always think and look before you leap
Something for the morrow fail not to keep
For the rainy day and contingency you save
to provide and feed the ones you dearly love.

One's purse will never be totally bare
if he knows well when to spend and spare
Spare the cent, the dollar will secure itself
Provide for the worst, tomorrow will save itself.

Thrift is the basis of savings and funds
Being lavish and extravagant incur debts
Always spend on needs and practise thrift
Industry is fortune's right hand, frugality her left.

They who save first become lenders
They who spend first turn to be borrowers
The lenders as providers form the ruling minority
who pitilessly shackle the poor, borrowing majority.

Money follows you not when you're called
but certainly essential in all matters figured
Remember you got to have enough of it though
even as your breath stops and you have got to go.

"Hope is the thing with feathers that perches in the soul and sings the tune without the words and never stops… at all"
- Emily Dickinson

44

Rainbow Of Hope

*"The hopeful look forward to a better future.
The hopeless, it does not matter anymore"*

No matter how strong the whirling storm
No matter how swift the gushing flood
However distant the targeted destination
However formidable the mission assigned.

Far above the clouds shines a shimmering star
A rainbow surely appears in every person's life
A silver lining in every cloud will also show up
As hope and promise of a better bright future.

Sometimes the sun shines, sometimes rain pours
It takes both the sun and rain to make a rainbow
A treasure awaits you at the foot of the rainbow
One can't say how close you're, but you're there.

As you reach the point where the rainbow ends
It drifts away like the mirage in a desert
That's the time your mind says it's enough
Let me pack up and leave, perhaps it isn't mine.

But if you focus closely, it's just one step away
You will definitely grasp that, you wish to hold
If you insist you aren't leaving till you possess it
You will certainly find the invaluable pot of gold.

DEATH AND DIGNITY

Quotes By Author

"Death is a destined reality that strikes lives
anyway, anyhow, anytime, anywhere: underground;
on the land; in the waters; in the sky; and even in space.
It awaits mankind at battlefields, highways, racing tracks,
plane routes, tunnels, prisons, hospitals, homes and everywhere"

"Suicide is man's way of expressing - enough is enough, I withdraw"

"Birth and death, in the hands of the Divine.
Only the life you live is in your hands"

==

"As dreams are made on,
our little life is rounded with a sleep"
William Shakespeare

"Detachment and Attachment
real parts of existence
Attachment with detachment
sets you apart,
gives you a bit of sad knowledge
…that accepts
the rose dying, the looks changing,
the words altering, friends parting
and finally Life itself"
Padma Chee (Whisperings)

"What is life that struts and frets upon the stage
and then is heard no more"
William Shakespeare

45

Fear Not Death

"Death is indisputably an absolute certainty
though man incessantly attempts to defy its inevitability"

Death is inevitable and indeed indispensable
No man has overwhelmed or defeated it
All attempts to evade it are of no avail
For sooner or later we'll be stung by it.

Life destined from a woman's womb
after all endeavours, end up in the tomb
No saint or scientist has found a remedy
or formula for an everlasting life on earth.

We tend to resist, fight and postpone death
knowing not at all that if we continue to hang
wriggling on the hook we'll be in agony forever
Death frees the soul from bondage and body.

The inevitable tragedy of our lives isn't
in aging, ailing, grieving, drowning or dying
But in what diminishes and alas dies inside us
while we still continue to resist and endure.

Why fret and fear that which is inevitable
While we are still breathing and kicking
we heed not the harbinger of death
When it strikes us, we are no more
Let it come, when it chooses.

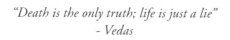

"Death is the only truth; life is just a lie"
- Vedas

46

Never The Same

*"You are no more only when you have been forgotten.
So long as you linger in the memory you're around"*

Sometimes sudden, other times gradual
Be it dreadful, peaceful or even natural
death takes away someone dearest to us
And causes untold grief and melancholy.

When death eventually embraces you
then you become a body with no capitals
Your existence here has become history
remembered by family and close associates.

It is said, death is a quickly forgotten episode
as your grief lasts only up to its departure
But to the very dearest and the closest this is
an eternal episode in their minds and hearts.

The tragedy of callous death plucks
your beloved away from the worldly scene
For most people life may go on as usual
but to the affected life is never the same again.

When alive, one is often taken for granted
but cherished when dead and gone for good
Remember to take time to be with aged parents
while they are around and more so when disabled.

"Stop fighting me. I am death"
- Anon

47

Anxiety Of Death

"Man fears death that creeps on him like a thief"

Both birth and death are beyond the control of man
In both occasions we can do nothing but wait anxiously
Their time of arrival and departure can never be known
Is there anyone who is capable of prophesying this?

He who is gravely ill and on the brink of death
breathes shallow and is not at all the person he was
Thoughtless of the loss of his dignity we won't let him go
Can the dying make a choice between living and dying?

It's a pity indeed the partially unconscious, the comatose
and paralysed suffer agony and misery but mostly loneliness
They prolong hopelessly with the empathy of the family
Can euthanasia be legalised to relieve their misery?

As man's physical health and mental capacity deteriorates
dying becomes a problem causing increased anxiety
Medication extends and teases his purposeless life, in drags
Doctors earnestly keep man going, but at what cost?

There will always be unfinished work, responsibilities and
aspirations at whatever age one leaves this world for good
All commitments, duties and activities must come to a stop
How long should a mortal being remain attached to this earth?

48

Who Called Me?

"Birth begins and death concludes.

Who called me to this earth
I know not from where
and for what purpose
I was brought here?

Who sang the lullabies
and rocked me
in the cradle
and lulled me to sleep?

Who led me to school
to be stuffed
with facts and figures
and take tests?

Who captured my heart
in matrimony
and drove me to bed
to blend into one?

Who called me lovingly
Papa and Daddy
and showered me
with love and care?

My time is up now
Even if I'm assured of heaven
I wish not to leave now
Should I be hesitant?

WHOM SHALL I CALL, NOW!

49

Passers-By

"Your birth can be a destined episode.
Make your life historic and your death a loss"

We devote and sacrifice
our time for service
We shower and share
all our love and care.

We sweat and compete
with all our might
We toil and slog
struggle and strive to excel.

We plan and scheme
to accomplish as a team
We split to go our ways
to be top of all others.

We argue and belittle
condemn and quarrel
We conflict and clash
All for comfort and cash.

We negotiate and deal
to own things or people
In the final countdown
we own nothing nor anyone.

All vices and virtues
all liabilities and assets
we leave behind and sigh
We are but mere passers-by.

WHAT CAN WE TAKE ALONG NOW!

*"No amount of tears, pleas or prayers can
awaken the dead and gone"*

50

Perfect Rest

"The moment man begins life, he starts counting his days.
Is it to die and vanish that he is born in this world?"

We strive, toil and risk
our lives to amass wealth
We die a thousand deaths
in the midst of our ventures.

Death is not negotiable nor
lends to any compromise
It comes sooner or later
Today me, tomorrow you.

Naked indeed, we are born
We die and leave naked
That's the naked truth
What did we bring to take?

Pleasure and pain are but
a passing phase in our life
Death to all human beings
a true fact, is perfect rest.

Our enlightened souls
go to the Almighty's abode
Let our organs intact
go to our needy fellow beings.

HUMANITY AND HUMILITY

Quotes By Author

"Humankind alone: bestowed with intelligence and intellect;
gifted with feelings of affection and compassion and endowed
with smile and laughter is the most blessed species on this planet"

"Life in this world is like endlessly moving clouds and sea waves.
What remain with us are the memories of moments that touched us"

"You are you, I am I, and if we can respect each other's ways,
this world will be a paradise with a peaceful and happier human race"

"Pride and grace will never go together.
He that humbles himself shall be uplifted and elevated eventually"

"If there's anything more than success and satisfaction, it's happiness-
being happy for others and most of all keeping yourself happy"

"Happiness in life is in a benevolent, caring relationship
which is by and large mutual and there are no two ways about it"

============================

"There is no path to happiness; happiness is the path"
Gautama Buddha

"Patience and the mulberry leaf becomes silk"
Chinese Proverb

"Charity sees the need not the cause"
German Proverb

51

Courtesy Maketh Man

*"Good mannerism and gentility are the noble traits of yesteryears
that are slowly being buried in the sands of time"*

Let your words be like sugar or nectar
Sweet, felicitous and musical to the ears
Pleasant, pleasing and soothing to the heart
Harmonious, delightful and blissful to the soul.

Small everyday courtesies sweeten life
A little kindness can make one feel better
There is blessing for service to needy mankind
rendered with utmost empathy and compassion.

You may be unable to solve the problems
troubles and miseries of the ones in distress
At least you can attempt to talk people out of
their depression, dejection and downheartedness.

The courtesy and kindness you can show
defer nor neglect not for whatever reason
You may not get to meet someone once again
or pass this fabulous planet earth in another life.

When you wish one a very good morning
lights of heaven will shine auspiciously on you.
When you wish one good night and sweet dreams
the angels in the heaven will give you peaceful sleep.

"Happiness springs from the experience of the creative wild leap of imagination"
- Anon

52

Gift Of Happiness

*"A happy and compassionate heart is richer than
a charming face or a big bank balance"*

Happiness as a matter of fact
certainly not a privilege or right
It's neither inherited nor bestowed
but a delightful state to be realised.

It comes not from luxury, riches
comfort, status, fame or praises
Instead it is derived from doing
all that are joyful and satisfying.

Happiness cannot be multiplied
unless it is plainly expressed
like love shared in a relationship
or goodwill nurtured in friendship.

The roots of bliss grow deepest
in the soil of an altruistic heart
The heart that beats for others
is the most blessed of all hearts.

May your future in every way
be blessed with wonderful days
of delight, fun, cheer and laughter
That you may live happily ever after.

53

The Magic Of A Smile

"Impeccable grooming is incomplete without a smile"

A smile is indeed an exclusive gift bestowed
upon human beings alone amongst all lives
A smile happens in just a flash of moment
while its fragrance lingers on and lasts long.

It is the best gesture during an acquaintance
as it pleases the eyes and lifts the spirit
A smile is a natural and effective opener for
a speech, a talk, a conversation and a request.

Many a tough man known to be indifferent
has melted at a pleasant, cheery, sweet smile
A smile promotes gaiety and serenity at home
and fosters goodwill at work and everywhere.

If anyone is unable or cannot give you a smile
do not hesitate to cheer him up with a smile
Probably life has exhausted him of joy and fun
Obviously he is in dire need of an inspiring smile.

It's a relieving prescription for the troubled
and the very best tonic for promoting friendship
It cheers up the lonely, the weary, the downhearted
the dejected and sheds light on the totally hopeless.

54

Patience Pays

"Patience is the panacea for the mounting
pressures and anxieties in today's rat race on earth"

Waiting is weary, tiring and tarrying
It consumes our cool and our patience
It drifts away our precious moments
and keeps us tensed and anxious.

Crawling in slow-moving traffic
Waiting in a long or sluggish queue
You can grumble, you are in a hurry
but do remember, so are the others.

Those who just cannot wait to watch
the buds bloom and the fruits ripen
Time trots for them in slow motion
Watch the kettle, it seems not to boil.

He attains who waits with patience
like the calm stork that meditates
on one leg for hours, only to take
a good bite of its unsuspecting prey.

Our life itself, from birth to death
is one long wait, none knows when
Everything comes to him who waits
Patience resolves all things to the end.

55

Diplomacy And Tact

*"Diplomacy like relationship in life is mutual
and there's no two ways about it"*

Set a thief to catch another thief
Beat the cunning at his own tricks
Remove a thorn with another thorn
Inject snake poison to treat a snake bite.

Lose a worm to catch a fish
Lose a battle and win the war
Throw the grains to catch the pigeons
Sometimes the best gains come after losses.

He who laughs last, laughs best
The last to come is often the master
The champion reserves the master blow
He knows enough that can hold his peace.

Fair and softly goes long and far
Children listen to music more than advice
Persuasion works much better than compulsion
There's great force inherent in love and empathy.

The way to a fair lady's heart is to sweeten her ears
The way to a gentleman's heart is to massage his ego
To win your bosses attention, make his priorities yours
Diplomacy is an art of making a point without causing hurt.

56

The Heart That Gives

"He lives who gives, he exists who receives"

The sun provides sunshine and solar energy
The rain pours water for cleansing and thirst
The tree gives shade, fruits, sap and wood
The cow ploughs, gives milk, cheese and meat.

We make a living with what we earn and use
Life is meaningful when we provide charitably
What is good, do it today while you're around
so that others may observe and emulate you.

The heart that is noblest of all hearts is one
that shows love and expresses compassion
Parting with benevolence to elevate the poor
without any publicity or expectations, is giving.

There is nothing nobler than a generous heart
The more you give, the more you share
Who gives not, is not living but merely existing
The more you impart, the more you're blessed.

A compassionate heart gives with no expectation
The left hand is unaware of that given by the right
The greatest blessing is bestowed upon the hands
that reach out to colour the lives of others in need.

*"Faith and persistence is the hope and
assurance for survival and success"*

57

A Better Tomorrow

*"You can't stop the 'ups and downs' in life
but you can learn to adapt to them"*

When you're extremely depressed, down and low
you attempt relentlessly to rewind and rebound
so as to start anew with vigour but to no avail
You obviously feel disappointed and hopeless.

When your mind is intricately perplexed
Your lofty and tender heart is gravely hurt
Your courage shrinks and drops to the lowest
and your determination slides to rock bottom.

Forget not, there is still faith that instills hope
charging with strength, confidence and passion
Without faith one is merely existing, not living
Faith is the panacea for an auspicious future.

Problems choke and fear haunts incessantly
Your confidence is shaken to the lowest level
Remember the silver lining in the dark cloud
Time is the hope for solution of all misfortunes.

There is no other motivation as effective as
the positive expectation of a better tomorrow
Submit and surrender yourself totally to the Almighty
This is the time the divine will begin to shine inside you.

"Happiness and satisfaction in the heart
pave the path for peace and harmony in the soul"

58

Satisfaction Is Bliss

*"Accomplishment is the basis of satisfaction
and the happiness that follows it"*

Man born ignorant, innocent and humane
turns ambitious, selfish and avaricious
He manoeuvres, manipulates and mollifies
to fulfill his heart's desire and infinite wishes.

His wants seem challenging and formidable
till he accomplishes and achieves them
Once obtained and possessed, his heart craves
for more and greater than that attained.

One should decisively determine his needs
Keep his desires and wants within limits
Otherwise, his looming evils will invade him
and most certainly destroy his poise and peace.

A day of honest work earns blessings of the divine
Sharing joy is a great feeling, too good to dismiss
Let it be food, celebration, duty of whatever design
will brim your cup of life with incomparable bliss.

End of the day it's not merely living a satisfactory life
but a feeling of utmost satisfaction in life, that matters
Its fulfilment and contentment, happiness and modesty
that bring peace and serenity to one's life on this earth.

CAUSALITY AND DESTINY

<u>Quotes By Author</u>

"Only when you're caught, you're a culprit, till then you're innocent.
Truth invariably catches up with lies sooner or later"

"Bearing the consequences for deeds is the rule of life
as there is no escape from the outcomes of cause and effect"

"Avaricious desires and promiscuous temptations have caused
the downfall of many a man"

"No rumour without gossip; no repercussion without provocation"

"Life is enjoying and suffering the fruits of our actions"

"It's better to die fighting wrong and injustice than to live
compromising principles and values"

"I'm my own destiny as I myself design my destination"

"Self-centered people indifferent to atrocities and injustice
are equally liable to bear the sins as much as the offenders"

"He who acts scrupulously and steadfastly without fear or favour
is unlikely to err or regret"

"Birth and death are destined entrance and exit gateways.
Invariably you only have the option to steer the life you live - your way"

==================================

"Sweet mercy is nobility's true badge"
William Shakespeare

"Cause and effect, means and ends, seed and fruit cannot be severed"
Emerson

59

Reward And Penalty

"They who condemn vices and do wrong, live in sin lifelong"

Every action has its reaction
Good begets good, evil begets evil
Every cause brings forth its outcome
Blessings bestow bliss, curses inflict pain.

Virtues and ethics are angels
Vices and immoralities are devils
Virtues comply and abide by consent
Vices usually differ and defy one another.

What seems lucrative and promising
is a mere illusive path leading to deception
The wicked and unscrupulous may flourish
and prosper but only until the truth surfaces.

As innocent victims of the underworld
we are unable to combat crooks and crime
Rehabilitation and restoration are the only
feasible medication to chasten brutal criminals.

In the final analysis, we're the sum total
of our own thoughts, feelings and actions
Our activities and operations reflect our life
Heaven ensures, no man scores bliss from crime.

"What goes around comes around like an echo and boomerang"

60

Boomerang

"Right wrongs no man; wrong saves no man"

He that handles thorns can prick his fingers
He that indulges in vices shall be in suffering
He that digs the pit, will fall into it, some day
He hurts himself, who wrongs others heartlessly.

He that respects not, is in turn not respected
As you think of others, others will think of you
He who blows upon the dust, fills his eyes with it
When one spits against the wind, he smears his face.

For industrialisation, agriculture is sacrificed
For modernisation, the environment is destroyed
High risks bigger profits, low risks lesser returns
Bigger the investment, greater is the remuneration.

What costs nothing is worth examining
What comes easy and quick may not stay long
Great haste saves no time instead makes great waste
Reckless drivers are likely victims of fatal accidents.

He that works till the sun sets, eats a hearty meal
He that toils day and night fails not to fill his rice bowl
He that dwells in pleasures, exhausts his fortune in no time
He that swells in prosperity, shall shrink in adversity sometime.

*"Variety is the very essence of life, that spices and
flavours the ways of the human race"*

61

Bitter Sweet Symphony

*"There can't be anything more boring than uniformity
in all people and things in this world"*

The aborigines who are the genuine natives of the soil
whether Red Indians or Maoris, they merely survive
The immigrants more in numbers, and very enterprising
usurp to reign over the ignorant and primitive natives
Isn't it the number that ultimately matters and counts?

Some traditions and culture permit man to take a few wives
provided he treats them equally, fairly and just
Others disapprove polygamy and bigamy altogether
Men dominate and determine, women sacrifice and please
Don't the privileges of men spell the predicament of women?

To some Hindus, the cow is considered a sacred animal
beef is forbidden meat hence a taboo to them
For some Muslims, the beef is much desired and very special
but pork is strictly forbidden dish in their meals
Shouldn't preferences and differences be respected?

Always barefooted the Buddhist enters the temple
chanting his prayers and rendering his devout service
The Christian walks into the church smartly dressed
for his sermon with shoes that are well polished and shining
Do different spiritual practices arouse conflicts or spice to life?

The ambitious are likely to get higher and higher in life
if they can keep their feet firmly and strongly to the ground
Dodgy and dubious leaders quickly get to the top of the rung
but thoughtlessly and heedlessly kick the ladder away
Aren't the stranded left too high on the cliff to access the ground?

"Damn the wheel of the world! Why must it continually turn over?
Where is the reverse gear
- Jack London 1876 - 1916

62

It's Time

"Time and Patience resolve problems and heal misgivings"

Truth should never be buried or hidden away
In time it will emerge bigger than life to pursue you
Simple things in life bring you the most happiness
In fact they come free and exist all around you.

So you have accumulated excess wealth over time
It's time to share with and care for the deprived
You have grown tall and big in your industry
It's time you come down to educate and share.

When threats, violence and irrational acts unbolt
it's time to retreat, but don't submit or revolt
If confronted and accused, unfair or baseless
it's time to voice out and fight for all your rights.

Laughter and smiles are man's unique inherent gifts
Let your hair down and enjoy the benefits in full
There's time for everything in life for better or worse
The choice is yours and the consequences too.

Time waits not nor does it tarry for your decisions
Lose or waste not, for you cannot catch it again
Do not allow it to consume you nor overtake you
Strive to engrave your name on the timeless screen.

"The human being is the greatest miracle of miracles"

63

Greatest Of Miracles

"A forthright and selfless man
is a miracle indeed in today's world"

The creator of this wonderful universe designed
nature and species with the essentials for coexistence
HE bestowed the human race uniquely with intellect
rationale, feelings and senses to lead a truly meaningful life.

Water, fire, earth, ether and air with all the inherent gases
in the correct proportion for lives to survive, is no accident
All species, especially lives and plants exchange oxygen with
carbon dioxide for existence, an astonishing marvel of nature.

The rise of water from the seas as clouds that return
to the ground as rain water is no work of a technocrat
No meteorologist can create or stop lightning and thunder
No scientist can invent sunlight and water for trees and lives.

All that inventors are able to innovate are life-like robots
Human cloning can create a genetic twin but never with a soul
nor implant in it a mechanism to breathe, think, feel or express
No innovator, sage or saint till now, is capable of creating life.

Interconnection and combination of all forces of nature
are astounding, mysterious formula for the survival of all species
In the chart of lives, what an amazing and unique creation man is
His intellect and ingenuity make him a marvellous miracle on earth.

"What a marvelous world of enchanting nature and blessed lives!"

64

Marvellous World

"The most wonderful gift to man is life on earth"

What a magnificent sight the world is!
The Amazon greenery, the Babylon Gardens
Mount Everest, the Alps, the Andes, the Glaciers
and the Niagara Falls are enchanting gifts of nature.

The twinkling stars, the colourful rainbow
The melodious joyful larks and the graceful fawn
The glittering fireflies, the shimmering sea animals
So soothing and pleasant to the eyes, ears and heart.

Out of all the fascinating creatures in nature
the humankind, the most intelligent of the lot
has carved out remarkable marvels and wonders
Human ingenuity has shaped the world to what it is today.

The Roman Colosseum, the Taj Mahal of India
The Great Wall of China and the Egyptian Pyramids
The mega complexes, bullet trains, rockets, radars
supercomputers and satellites are all amazing creations.

The historical landings on Moon and Mars are
but just the beginning of more discoveries of mankind
But unlike the giving nature, man leaves vast destruction
in his success trails of flabbergasting wonders and marvels.

65

Enjoy Your Stay

*"It matters not why you exist, but the fact that you're already here,
live life fruitfully to the fullest and that's what matters"*

Why we are here, is an unresolved question
probed by mankind from time immemorial
There is nothing that we can do about it
but live purposefully the life bestowed upon us.

Though we aren't sure of our purpose here
we definitely can be positive in our approach
We need to understand our unlimited power
and sense the thirst that dwells in us to shine.

Birth after birth here, isn't mere tribulation
but exposure that enriches ones' experiences
in communicating with mankind and nature
Gifted are souls that take on life on this planet.

Sweet memorable dreams in a peaceful sleep
A joyful shower under a lovely cool waterfall
Listening to one's favourite melodious music
All these give immeasurable pleasure and joy.

Life is indeed a wonderful journey of possibilities
Man alone explores all avenues of his existence
using his ingenuity to grab nature's invaluable gifts
Whatever the task, do it but make a difference.

66

Destiny

*"Providence creates events and episodes with reason
shifting one's destiny to unexpected directions"*

Life is a race, hiking to the top
Some are striding up and riding high
Others, sliding down and feeling wry
The rest stand aside, just pondering.

When victory has decided
the appropriate time to embrace you
destiny puts everything in place
to complete the job for you.

When misfortune has aptly fixed
its timely hour to entrap you
fate will create temptations
to entice you to venture and lose.

The world is but a checker board
We are all mere tiny pawns
moved by the invisible hand
Destiny makes the vital move.

The greatest mystery in life is
Not knowing what is awaiting next
Why worry about what you know not
What has to happen inevitably happens.

BELIEF AND FAITH

Quotes By Author

"When the stomach is full, we say 'no more', it's enough.
For materialistic matters we say 'some more', it isn't enough.
To advise, we give a deaf ear and say 'not anymore', please!
For love and affection our heart yearns for more and more.
When is it actually enough for the inordinate humankind?"

"Challenge yourself and change with time
to stand out with proactive go-getters and achievers"

"Great minds have foresight and insight.
Little minds have yearnings and longings"

"Belief and faith in hope is the final straw to hang on to,
for better times in life"

"Anything that is not based on evidence and proof
will find solace in the belief system"

"End of the day the most important person to you in your life
is none other than you yourself"

"He is blessed indeed who is an inspiration
and a lighthouse to fellow mankind groping in ignorance"

"Intention becomes meaningful when it has a higher purpose.
Action turns out noble when performed as a benevolent service"

===============================

"Faith is a bird, that can see the light when it is dawn
and starts singing in the dark"
Rabindranath Tagore

"There is enough for everyone's need but not for everyone's greed"
Mahatma Gandhi

67

Belief Is Absolute Faith

"Belief and faith are inspiring forces of life that drive one
to persevere and finish the race"

You very well can take on a mission
work with passion and realise your vision
You can set your goals and attain the targets
All with faith and belief in your heart.

You think 'out of the box', offer solutions
even to formidable obstacles and problems
You can overwhelm any crisis, confidently
All with faith and belief in your ingenuity.

You can overturn a critical misfortune
to immeasurable, invaluable goldmine
You can convert failure to opportunity
All with faith and belief in intellectuality.

You can execute whatever you attempt
with full involvement and commitment
Take on, however tough, with conviction
Faith and belief relieve all that is forbidden.

You can be free from insecurity and crime
You can change bad time to blessed time
You can transform deficiency into competency
All done with faith and belief in your persistency.

68

Believing Versus Knowing

"Faith begins where intelligence ends"

Believing is based on absolute faith that convinces one
to believe that formless things exist as energy or spirit
Knowing is seeing, grasping and comprehending
facts and figures before our naked eye.

All things seen, smelt, touched, tasted
heard, sensed and experienced seem so real
As in all scientific and clinical experiments, anything
tangible and provable has to be based on evidence.

Astrology, palmistry, prophesies, all occult arts
baffling supernatural and esoteric mysticism
are beyond the ordinary man's logic and measures
Truly a phenomenal world of the paranormal.

Superstitions, supposition and theologies
may prompt one to believe and to readily justify
Did man create God to dump all his fears and the
inexplicable phenomena to this unknown source?

Only when man discerns the naked truth
from the beliefs handed down by his ancestors
over time immemorial, he realizes his true role on earth
which defines a balance between believing and knowing?

69

Change With Changes

"It's not the most brilliant or toughest but the one most
responsive to change who perseveres and prospers in life"

Birth, death and change are three basic constants in life
All living species including the human race, the climate
vegetation, nature, the environment and everything else
without exception undergo change from time to time.

The world is changing rapidly and those who remain
chained to myths and superstitions are left way behind
Those ever ready to adopt and adapt to change in life
obviously progress and make headway with time.

The nature, habits, beliefs and lifestyle of mankind
change and are rapidly changing for better or worse
Economy takes priority over everything else now
Even agriculturists readily turn into industrialists.

Man has to first build his home and nurture his family
It's with mutual respect and sacrifice a family survives
He has to attune himself with the new wave of changes
but not without compromising his ancient golden values.

Man has the inherent power to change and transform
hence with intelligence steer his life in the right direction
End of the day he should live a life without any regret
that would speak of his altruistic service to fellow mankind.

"I took the road less travelled by, and that has made all the difference"
- Robert Frost

70

Choice Is Yours

"Life is forever about decisions, advances and compromises"

You want to realise your dream and vision
Set your mission with a direction and passion
Or daydream, laze and wander around
seeking reasons to remain conveniently idle?

You want to be in school to acquire knowledge
values and skills to live a meaningful worthy life
Or play truant, indulge in straying with bad company
teaming up to commit crime and ruin yourself?

You want to avoid cigarettes, alcohol, drugs
all health hazards to maintain a healthy lifestyle
Or succumb to temptations that override discipline
tempting you to taste and alas get addicted?

You want to clear up debts and overcome poverty
with diligence, skill, ingenuity and honest earnings
Or indulge in burglary, drug trafficking and crime
earning imprisonment and lifetime misery?

You want to change with time and make things happen
or stand and watch prospects slowly slip away
Your life is your choice and is certainly in your hands
Come to think of it, you will live a life you deserve.

71

I Know Not

"All that beyond knowledge and comprehension of man, remain unresolved mysteries of the world"

I know after winter comes spring
I know every cloud has a silver lining
I know the bud soon blooms into a flower
I know a rich harvest is subject to good weather.

I know lightening is followed by thunder
I know we are shielded by the ozone layer
I know the stars are visible only in the night
I know when the sun shines the sky turns bright.

I know that there is no gain without pain
I know there is no mission without a vision
I know there is no such thing as a free meal
I know that there is no business without a deal.

I know that a chain breaks at its weakest link
I know those who are extravagant will soon sink
I know nothing travels more swiftly than scandal
I know that our mortal life in this world is a gamble.

I know that the days of youth are the days of glory
I know when eyes meet they conclude in matrimony
I know we have descended to live a life on this planet
I KNOW NOT how long man's illusions and delusions last!

72

A Burden

*"Attach not yourself to strong sentiments for they are mere
transient elements that drop off when time is ripe"*

A dream is a burden when there is no vision
A vision is a burden when there is no mission
A mission is a burden when there is no direction
A direction is a burden when there is no passion.

The heart is a burden when there is no love
Beauty is a burden when there is no grace
Love is a burden when there is no mutual trust
A marriage is a burden when there is no sacrifice.

A relationship is a burden when there is no bonding
Responsibility is a burden when there is no caring
Friendship is a burden when there is no benevolence
A family is a burden when there is no harmony.

Life is a burden when there is no happiness
Religion is a burden when there is no faith
Humanity is a burden when there is no compassion
The world is a burden when there is no law and order.

You are to yourself a burden when there's no initiative
You are to others a burden when there's no self-sustenance
The body to the soul is a burden when there's no renunciation
The soul to itself is a burden when there's no enlightenment.

DIVINITY AND ALMIGHTY

Quotes By Author

"Religion as a matter of fact enables the human soul to dispel ignorance,
lead a just and spiritual life, seek divinity and ultimately attain enlightenment"

"Animosity amongst religions are arousing dire conflicts all around the world.
They've become powerful tools segregating mankind into global fanatical followers.

"Disputes between religions occur more often than their debates with atheists"

"Religions should erect bridges of harmony instead of walls of controversies.
Religion is divine when it unites. Religion is no more religion when it divides"

"The Almighty God is the solace for the disheartened and downhearted
who are probing and groping in the dark for solution and salvation"

"Absolute unity of the human race is not purely in religion, race,
language, culture or status but more crucially in the loving heart"

"The Supreme Being, worshipped in whatever form or formless state
is absolutely One and the Same to all lives"

==

"The essence of all religions is one. Only their approaches are different"
Mahatma Gandhi
"Men will wrangle for religion, write for it, die for it anything but live for it"
Charles Colton
"Religion is opium of the masses"
Karl Marx

"Religion bridges God and man"
African Proverb
"Know Thyself"
Socrates

73

Question Of Evolution

"Can we attribute all existence to an unknown source?"

Did man come first or the woman
Did the seed come first or the tree
Did the egg come first or the chicken
Did the caterpillar come first or the butterfly.

Hi man! What are you-a force, soul or energy
What's your link to this earth and the Creator
For what purpose are you brought to this world
Did you bring yourself here to discover your SELF.

Our blue planet a spin off from the sun, blazed
boiled and raged for years changing and changing
Dust, water, aqua plants and living cells over time
transform miraculously making way to the birth of man.

Yet again by Darwin's evolution, he says
Apes have evolved to be today's human race
That being so, why are some apes still apes
What mystery shrouds this controversial theory.

Whence and why this universe, the species
the flora and fauna emerge on the face of earth
And man himself unique among all living creatures
Wherefore the unknown Source's Hand in this creation.

"Beware the demon in disguise for she carries the seed of destruction
in her pretty bosom"
- Anon

74

Demons In Disguise

"Hell is deserted as all the sinners are here.
Heaven is closed for none so worthy of being there"

Religious fanaticism and radicalism pose as
one of the greatest perils to human civilization
A threat indeed to fraternity amongst mankind
and peace amongst nations on this planet earth.

Fanatics pull down shrines of other faiths
to replace their own places of worship
A sacred, costly competition indeed
to shelter a homeless God.

Persecution of religious critics
Is often justified by orthodox flag bearers
Open academic inter-religious conversations
turn unpleasant, too sensitive and intolerable.

Atheists, agnostics, disbelievers, freethinkers, cynics
particularly critics of dogmatic religious doctrines
labelled devils and trouble makers are condemned
to hell, banished or even persecuted.

Religious crusades and genocides supposedly
pursued in the name of retrieving the holy lands
and safeguarding their followers and doctrines but
at what cost of human lives and civilisations on earth.

75

Hypocritical Exploits

*"Manipulating and maneuvering religion for ulterior motives
will only end up with undesirable consequences"*

Liquor and cigarettes asserted as injurious
to health, made available openly in public places
Ill-gotten monies from illicit practices, deposited
privately in tight security offshore funds and banks
Nuclear weaponries long condemned and forbidden
But preserved for self-defense and reciprocal peace.

Religious radicals race to pinch followers
and effectually convert them to their faiths
A practice conducted with the pretext of taking
the converts on the supposedly right path to God
Isn't the essence of all religions invariably, spiritualism.

Religions deeply obsessed with conversion
distribute handouts to increase their numbers
It's conversion of vices to virtues; chaos to peace
oppression to liberation and negativity to positivity
that can convert the world to a better place to live.

Religions in the guise of selling us heaven
invariably keep us firmly embedded in hell
We are neither to rationalise nor question but
simply abide by their absolute dogmatic doctrines
Perhaps it's wiser to listen than to question doctrines.

When others err, we condemn them as malicious
When we do wrong, it is an unintentional mistake
A true man says what he does and does what he says
Out of conflict with others, we readily resort to battles
Out of conflict within us, we feign to be philosophers.

76

Wishes Of The Great One

*"More blessed are the hands that are stained in service
and charity than those that are clasped in worship and prayer"*

Is the Almighty Lord interested to know whether
You're an African, an Asian, an Arab or a European
You converse in English, French, Japanese, Mandarin
Or if you are caring, compassionate and loving to all lives.

Is the Supreme Being concerned to check whether
You're a celebrity, an upstart, a master or a servant
You're an entrepreneur, an executive, a wage earner
Or if you are acting with a conscience and accountability.

Is the All pervading Omniscient eager to observe whether
You're literate or illiterate, knowledgeable, smart or naive
You're an intellectual, a philosopher, a mastermind, a jester
Or if you uphold values, morals, righteousness, law and order.

Is the All mercy Omnipresent keen to watch whether
You are a heavyweight, lightweight, Hercules or Lilliput
You're a superman, a layman, an incumbent, an underdog
Or if you are that humane human, HE envisages you to be.

Is the All powerful Omnipotent longing to view whether
You can reach out to the distant stars or remain on earth
Discover the underworld, explore the universe, outer space
Or if you sincerely heed his golden message 'live and let live'.

"We are only puppets. Our strings are being pulled by unknown forces"
-Geog Buchaner: 1813-1837

77

Creation For Recreation!

*"No human complete with all his senses, wisdom and
spirituality is capable of fully understanding God"*

Who am I in this sensitive perishable body
For what reason am I brought here to this planet
Is it my asking and earnest wish to be here on earth
Did I beg YOU for a life to experience joy and suffering.

YOU are the Artist, I'm your minute art piece
YOU are the Poet, I'm your plain and simple poem
YOU are the Director, I'm your obedient, dutiful actor
YOU are the Player, I'm your little pawn pushed around.

YOU have bestowed me with priceless senses
I can see, smell, relish, hear, feel, think and relate
Yet ambition, temptation and greed override discipline
I am easily enticed to blunder, bungle, mistake and slip.

All pleasures and entertainment are short-lived
Anxiety and worry; agony and misery; fear and fright
tragedy and insecurity; disease and old age loneliness
Why should I suffer these torments and pain in this life.

Am I YOUR plaything, to fox-trot to YOUR tune
Whosoever offered this mortal physique to my soul
I plead to YOU to end this conjuring play, once and for all
Delight not in utilising YOUR creation for YOUR recreation.

"Unity in Divinity is the topmost priority for harmony in humanity"

Source: <u>donsnotes.com/religion/index</u>.html

78

The One And Only

*"The Almighty God is the one and only source of all
that was, that is and that will be"*

God, Lord, Allah, Sri Krishna, Siva, Bhagavan or Jehovah
The Supreme Being, Almighty, the Divine or the Great One
Whatever the image, form or formless state, God is worshipped
Are they or they aren't different names of the one and the same?

Be it HIS: incarnation - Sri Rama; son - Jesus Christ
Prophets – Buddha, Muhammad, Bahaullah or Guru Nanak
They emerged on earth at various periods to enlighten mankind
Are they or they aren't holy messengers from the one and the same?

Mankind is bestowed with an invaluable treasure of wisdom
The Vedas, the Bhagavad Gita, the Al-Quran, the Bible, the Torah
the Tantaras, the Zend-Avesta, the Talmud and all holy scriptures
Are they or they aren't sacred revelations of the one and the same?

Some theologians argue that only their religious doctrines
creeds, tenets, forms of worship and spiritualism is absolute
They act as the chosen lot endowed with the blessing of Divinity
Has God given anyone the right to be HIS spokesman on this planet?

With similarities, men tend to care and share and be united
With differences they disassociate, disintegrate and fall apart
All religions fundamentally preach love, peace, morals and unity
Religions are many and vary, God is absolutely one and the same.

"Prayer takes you to God.
Meditation brings God to you"

79

Reaching The Almighty

"When you are lost yourself, can you find God?"

Conception and perception of God are many
Religious faith, beliefs, and relief are many
Dogmas, doctrines, studies and scrutinies vary
Prophets, theologians, ascetics speak of but ONE.

Some see divinity in creation
Others set eyes on images and pictures
The rest look beyond and perceive infinite power
Who is to awaken us to the naked truth.

I hear sermons, hymns, chants and mantras
I see people meditate, fast, do penance and offerings
I still don't see the purpose and the consequence
I vouch that my conscience is my only faith.

No matter what belief, faith or practice
whichever religion man chooses, they all unequivocally
point to the ONE and only, revered in various names
The ONE who reigns the universe, nature and all of us.

Ethics, righteousness and compassion in man's deeds
are blissful traits that lead to consciousness and divinity
As much as all rivers meander to reach the sea
so do different faiths lead to the ONE supreme God
Man should be free to choose his wagon to attain HIM.

80

God's Religion

*"The Supreme God is in all faiths
that inculcate love, peace and unity in the human race"*

This religion or that
Theirs, yours, his and mine
Which religion or what religion
is the Almighty, Supreme Absolute GOD?

Hearing the joyful birds chirp and sing
man created music and symphonies
Seeing the intricate network of bees
he formed consumer marts.

What model did he see to create
a religion or recognise the sins we bear
What access has man to all sacred secrets
Yet he deteriorates and slips into sinful ways.

The Almighty has never been the problem
but some egocentric spiritual promoters
Blind faith and fanaticism are the two
facets of religion that trigger enmity.

Religious tolerance alone isn't the solution
Mutual religious respect, honour and regard
establishes harmony, reconciliation and peace
That's divinity in all religions of the human race.

81

What Next ?

*"Discovering your real 'Self' through the corporeal
roles is what spiritual enlightenment is all about"*

Modernization has tampered with nature
inciting climate change and global warming
Nations are not paying much heed to warnings
of consequent devastating natural calamities.

Civilized human race has attained the
pinnacle of material success on this planet
Now bent on barbarically annihilating each other
humankind has delved in search of a safer planet.

We arrive with nothing, strive for everything
live with something and leave without anything
Why stress ourselves tirelessly in this perishable
temporary station that we do not belong to at all.

Where do we go from here - to another planet
Reincarnate on this earth to live all over again
Wait till judgment day places us in heaven or hell
Linger as ghosts or return to the supreme God's abode.

Our prosperity and adversity are the doings of circumstances
Our reminiscences of the closest and dearest belong to time
Our material possessions and riches are interred in the earth
Our body to dust and our deeds to buff our soul to salvation
The greatest mystery is not knowing what is next in life and after life.

82

Life After Life

*"No matter what, learn to accept matters that cannot be changed.
Step aside and watch the drama rather than dramatizing it further"*

Karma – reincarnation is the fundamental doctrine of
Hinduism and Buddhism balancing vices and virtues
settling deeds dark and fair accumulated from past lives
to liberate and buff our souls to moksha or salvation.

Nobility or deformity, prosperity or adversity and
all episodes in the present life, are not mere coincidences
but destined karmic effects on mankind based on the
principle of cause and effect of their deeds during past lives.

Attachment and insatiable desires, prompt us to eagerly
and endlessly revolve in a mundane cycle of activities
and relationships losing ourselves in transient joys and funs
that consequently place us perpetually in worldly bondage.

They who forever pursue extreme pleasures and excitement
in the enticing worldly affairs will eventually come to realise
they are being enslaved in their pursuits without any means
to free or release themselves from the subsequent sufferings.

We are entangled very much with inconsistent worldly affairs
and inevitably face tribulations and disappointments that
lead to anxiety and tension causing dire distress and misery
If only we are aware of the nature and philosophy of karma!

Souls that depart from the dead bodies will be subjected
to a hearing conducted by the Masters in the Divine court
and subsequently take on the next befitting corporeal role
to redress the wrong and sins committed during past lives.

As birth and death revolves in unpredictable cycles, the soul
reincarnates and merges into another body in the next life
based on the experiences stored in the sub conscious mind
This process is repeated to reap the fruits of past lives.

Attachment and detachment; detachment and attachment
Only the modest and selfless soul with neither wild desires
nor expectations could possibly perceive a new world of
freedom totally unperturbed in the best and worst situations.

Only when negative and undesirable – reins are well secured
and contained, future manifestations may very well be in check
This cycle of birth, death and rebirth or reincarnation recurs
till our karmic accounts of past lives are completely neutralized.

Human experience ultimately leads to spiritual enlightenment
the acme of God – realization, total bliss, end of reincarnation
At the point of time of ultimate birthlessness and deathlessness
human soul-jeevatma unites with the Supreme Soul-Paramatma.

"Life is only a reflection of what we allow ourselves to see"
- Anon

To My Readers

What do you know of my toil?
Those coiling thoughts in my brain
Day and night arranging and rearranging
Again the thoughts return O! Deranging!
To pen or reject, I declare the stinging pain
Do the words speak or is my tireless reach foiled?

Will my readers be as amazed as me?
All I know every moment I deeply cherish
as I shape my words to weave my desired poetry
Not mere spilling of loose flourished emotion
drawn deep from my soul's experience directory
capturing the embedded thoughts that try to escape my mind.

Ponder again and again
No more, I lay my pen to rest
It's your turn to read
And put my life's ambition to test
My work is done
I had fun.

"Where there is peace, there is life"

Bibliography

1. Rees Nigel. Sayings of the Century. London: George Allen & Unwin, 1984.
2. Andres,Dr.Thomas Q . Quotes and Humor for Value Education.vol.1&2. Makati, Manila: St.Paul Publishings, 1987.
3. Timberlake, Lewis and Reed Marietta. Born To Win. Wheaton, Illinois: Tyndale House Publishers,Inc., 1980.
4. Peale, Norman Vincent. The Power of Positive Thinking. London: Vermillion, 1988.
5. Diwakar, R.R and Ramakrishnan, S(ed.). Immortal Words: an Anthology. Bombay: Bharatya Vidya Bhavan, 1990.
6. Johari, P. K. Social Conflicts. New Delhi: Anmol Pub., PVT.Ltd., 2007.
7. Gaspar Karl M. To be poor and obscure. Manila: Ctr. for spirituality, 2004.
8. Tyagi, Avinash. Climate change and global warming. New Delhi: Rajat Pub., 2006.
9. Gray, Colin S. War peace and International Relations: an introduction to strategic history. London: Routledge, 2007.
10. Kennnedy, Philip. Christianity: an introduction. London: I. B. Tauris, 2011.
11. Humphreys, Christmas (ed.)The wisdom of Buddhism. London: Curzon Press, i987.
12. Turner, Colin. Islam: the basics. 2nd ed. London: Routledge, 2001.
13. Hayes, Terrill. Life, death and immortality: the journey of the soul. 1st ed. Illinois: Bahai Pub., Trust, 1994.
14. Parthasarathy, A. Vedanta Treatise: the eternities.(Rev.ed.).Mumbai: A.Parthasarathy, 2004 .
15. Gulati, Mahinder N. Comparative religions and philosophies. New Delhi: Atlantic Publishers,Ltd., 2008.
16. Klemke, E.D. To believe or not to believe: readings on the philosophy of religion. Florida: Harcourt Brace Jovanovich College Pub., 1992.
17. Al-Attas, Syed Ali Tawik. A guide to philosophy. Subang Jaya. Malaysia: Pelanduk Pub., 2009.
18. Yogananda, Paramahansa. Wine of the mystic: The Rubaiyat of Omar Khayyam, a spiritual interpretation. Singapore: Self-Realisation Fellowship, 1994.
19. One Week Course: for attainment of complete purity, peace and prosperity. (Rev.ed.) Rajastan: BrahmaKumaris Ishwariya Vishwa Vidyaiaya, 1996.
20. Padma Chee . Ancient Whisperings, 2012.

Watch your thoughts; they become words
Watch your words; they become actions.
Watch your actions; they become habits.
Watch your habits; they become character.
Watch your character; it becomes your destiny.

Frank Outlaw

Selected Quotes By Author from the Poems

"A smile is an exclusive gift bestowed upon human beings alone"

"In life you are either a financial victor as a lender or a financial victim as a borrower"

"Living in debts is crueler than death. In its grip, you die a thousand deaths"

"He is blessed whose hands touch the lives of others. The heart that beats for others is the noblest of hearts"

"Truth should never be buried or hidden away. In time it will emerge bigger than life to pursue you"

"Your life is your choice and it's in your hands. Your thoughts and actions reflect your life"

"We strive and strain to attain all that we desire. End of the day we live a life that we deserve"

"Life is a race, hiking to the top. Some are striding up and riding high. Others are sliding down and feeling wry. The rest, stand aside, gazing and pondering"

"Born and raised in a very complex world; egg or chicken, seed or tree still puzzled; man lives thoroughly bewildered and departs utterly perplexed"

'We arrive with nothing; strive for everything; live with something; leave without anything. Why tire out in this temporary station, we don't belong to it at all"

"Man's intellect and ingenuity make him a marvelous miracle on earth"

S.Errakiah

148

Selected Quotes By Author from the Poems

"Love is a burden when there's no trust; religion is a burden when there's no faith"

*"As much as all rivers meander to reach the sea,
different faiths lead to the supreme God-Head"*

*"Did man create God to dump his fears and
inexplicable phenomena to this unknown source"*

*"Hi Almighty Divine ! Do I see the sparkle in Your eye
In steering Your humble creation for Your recreation?"*

*"This religion or that; yours, his and mine;
which religion reveals the Almighty God?
Isn't HE all religion and all religion HIM!"*

*"More than religious tolerance, its mutual respect
that nurtures spiritual harmony"*

*"I know we have descended to live a life on this planet.
I know not how long man's illusions and delusions will last"*

*"Why fret and fear over what is inevitable.
While we are still breathing and kicking,
we heed not the harbinger of death.
When it strikes us, we are no more"*

*"Does death transform us to lingering Ghosts
till Judgment Day place us in heaven or hell?
Reincarnate us in yet another drama here?
Return us to the Souls or God's abode?"*

*"The greatest mystery in life is, Not knowing what is awaiting next.
God is the Playwright. His play is man"*

S.Errakiah

Printed in the United States
By Bookmasters